# READER REVIEWS

**The following testimonials are from parents like you who read this book during its creation.**

*"I can see this book becoming a companion for those who find themselves on this unimaginable path of child loss. It is a wonderful acknowledgement of all that we endure in our first year of grieving".*
Carly Marie Dudley, Christian's mama

*"THIS is the book I wish I'd had the first year after my son died".*
Joy Borstein, Bennet's mama

*"This book provides the recognition that there is no one-size- fits-all and no set timeline for healing".*
April Gregoryk, Ethan's mama

*"A collection of heartfelt stories from loss parents that gives an authentic look into the trials and triumphs of the first year. It is at times tender, at times raw and at times humorous with one resounding message: you are not alone".*
Emily Wetherholt, Wyatt's mama

*"So many stories, all different, but somehow all the same".*
Jan Smith, Ben and Zach's mama

*"I am not new to grief; however, this book has been amazing for me. It has helped things come to light that I didn't realize were lingering and holding me back, has allowed me to understand so much more about healing and has given me hope".*
Laurel Taylor, Brianna's mama

# *Surviving*
## MY FIRST YEAR OF
# CHILD LOSS

### PERSONAL STORIES FROM GRIEVING PARENTS

**FOR THOSE EXPERIENCING PREGNANCY AND INFANT
LOSS, STILLBIRTH OR THE DEATH OF A CHILD**

# NATHALIE HIMMELRICH

**First Edition**

## Surviving My First Year of Child Loss: Personal Stories from Grieving Parents

By Nathalie Himmelrich
*A not-for-profit project by Grieving Parents Support Network*

ISBN 978-3-9524527-4-5

Cover Photograph: Michael Goh
Cover and Interior Design: Nada Assem
Dragonfly Art: Nathalie Himmelrich
Unattributed Quotes: Nathalie Himmelrich
Butterfly Art: Carly Marie Dudley
Publisher: Reach for the Sky

To access additional resources for parents and others grieving the loss of a baby or child, or for friends and family supporting them, visit **www.grievingparents.net**

For bulk purchases of *Surviving My First Year of Child Loss: Personal Stories from Grieving Parents,* contact **info@grievingparents.net**.

In honour of all babies and children gone too soon:

*Your Child*

*Alex*

*Amya Mirica, Rumi, Jai*

*Aveline Mae*

*Beau Christopher*

*Benjamin*

*Bradley David*

*Brendan, Cianan, Kavyn, Alex*

*Charlie*

*Daisy, Timothy, Titus, Sarah*

*Elizabetta*

*Ethan*

*Felix*

*Francesca*

*Georgia Jeanne*

*Grace*

*Isobel Olivia*

*James*

*Jensen Grey, Huxley*

*Karina*

*Luisa*

*Naomi Laura, Lil' Bub*

*Nathaniel Willis*

*Noel*

*Oliver Martin*

*Ryan*

*Sofia Noelle*

They are our reasons to never give up.

# INDEX

# CONTENTS

# PREFACE
## NOTE TO THE READER

We are sorry for the reason you have picked up this book: the loss of your baby or child. We are equally glad that you have found the courage, in the midst of your devastation, to read the offerings of others who have walked the same road and wish to express hope and comfort.

This book has been written for you by us, mothers and fathers who have experienced – and survived – the loss of our children. It is a collaborative, not-for-profit support resource for parents and those who support them after the loss of a baby or child. The following pages contain twenty-six essays that convey our individual challenges and the ways we coped during the first twelve months after the deaths of our children.

Much like Nathalie's book, *Grieving Parents: Surviving Loss as a Couple*, this book can be read at any point in your grief journey. It can be read chapter by chapter, or you can follow your intuition and read the section or essay that draws your attention. The essays include many different perspectives, and the book was compiled with respect for all cultural and religious identities. Themes and topics are listed in the index and table of contents. Choose a story that speaks to you and look for nuggets of wisdom that apply to you and your situation. Sentiments that do not apply to you and your unique story can be left aside.

We encourage you not to keep this book on your shelf, but to use it, make notes and pass it along to someone else who is grieving. Additional resources for parents and others grieving the loss of a baby or child can be found at www.grievingparents.net. The website also contains more information on each of the contributors to this book. If you wish to contact a contributor, please send an email to info@grievingparents.net and indicate to whom you are directing your message.

On behalf of the members of the worldwide Grieving Parents Support Network, we express our desire that you find whispers of hope and healing while reading this book. May it positively impact your journey of grief and healing. Above all, know that *you are not alone.*

*-- The Editorial Team*

This book uses British English spelling and grammar conventions.

# INTRODUCTION
## WHY THIS BOOK

I'm deeply sorry for the reason that brought you here to read this book. I am also glad you have found it.

Along with the community of bereaved parents, I embrace you into this club to which you never wanted to belong. Losing a child or a baby is a parent's worst nightmare. Each of us in this club has been there. I want you to know you are not alone. You can survive this, just as we have survived this.

This book is a messenger of Hope. Through this book, we, as bereaved parents, reach out to show you how we've found hope in the darkest hours that followed the loss of our children. We are here to show you ways in which we have managed the challenges we faced, some of which you might also face. We want to support you in believing in yourself and help you access your resilience in the moments when you lose faith.

We cannot take away your pain. We do not offer simple solutions. Simple solutions do not exist. Grieving the loss of our children is the most difficult and most courageous task we will ever undertake. There were times when we didn't know if we wanted to continue living: times when it all seemed too hard. Yet, we survived. We made it through. Our stories share the lessons we learned along the way and how we overcame the challenges. You can do this, too.

There is no way around grief. There are no shortcuts. The only way is through. We are here to show you the way through the challenges. We want to accompany you in your grief, and we will walk alongside you and hold your hand.

Much love,

*Nathalie*

# ACKNOWLEDGEMENTS
## WITH HEARTFELT THANKS

I want to first acknowledge all bereaved parents walking this path of life after loss. It requires an enormous amount of strength and resilience, which we never thought we had, and we find only while walking this path.

Some 300 mothers and fathers from the Grieving Parent Support Network global community originally expressed interest in taking part in this project. That, in and of itself, required enormous courage. I acknowledge your courage and thank you for your willingness to support others along this journey of child loss.

For all of you who submitted essays for consideration, that entailed the daunting task of looking within, revisiting the challenges of the first year and expressing the ways in which you helped yourselves during that time. You are brave; thank you for your courage.

The following bereaved parents have contributed to this edition: Alanna Salter, Alice R. Graham, Amanda Russell, Andrea Vurdea, Ariane Amann, Chiara Giommarelli, Chris Young, Christine Stabler, Danielle Ridgway, David Cooksey, Elizabeth Jones, Emily McEntire, Heather Strom, Julia Sorko, Karen Prisco, Katja Faber, Keem Schultz-Fares, Lindsey Lynch, Megan Warren, Rachel Libby, Rebecca Harris, Ryan Thompson, Samantha Medaglia, Sarah L. Hagge, Sophie McAulay and Tara Rigg. *Thank you for opening your heart.*

Special thanks go to Tim Morrison for editing and to Keem Schultz-Fares and Sarah L. Hagge for assisting with managing this project – without you it wouldn't have been possible. Thank you to our proofreaders and launch team, Michael Goh for cover photography, Nada Assem for cover and interior design and my friend Carly Marie Dudley for her heartfelt foreword.

Most of all, I wish to thank my own children. They remain the inspiration for everything I've created since they came into existence. I also acknowledge all the children whose stories haven't ended, even while their physical presence is sorely missed. Their names are not limited to those included within this book, but we name them on these pages in remembrance of all children who have died before their parents.

Nathalie Himmelrich

Founder, Grieving Parents Support Network

# FOREWORD
## THEY MATTER

Nothing throws us into an existential crisis quite like the death of a baby or child. Life is turned upside down and we are suspended between two worlds, the before and the after, while the rest of the world goes on as if nothing has happened. We torture ourselves with the whys and what ifs. We feel overwhelmed not knowing what to believe anymore. For most parents, there are no silver linings when it comes to new and raw grief: there is just pain and a deep yearning for everything to be different. Grief consumes every fibre of our being.

This book is a stunning collection of real, heart-breaking yet hopeful stories written by a community of bereaved parents who courageously share their first year of life – and how they coped – after the deaths of their children. They have all been devastated, some more than once, yet somehow, they breathe through their pain – and rise. They live their new lives with intention and meaning.

These parents come from different countries and backgrounds. They have different beliefs, interests, professions and relationship statuses. Their babies and children lived and died under different circumstances and yet, in all their diversity, they share one common bond: the love they feel for the children they can no longer hold in their arms. That kind of love shines bright and strong and will never be extinguished. While each story in this book may differ from yours, you will find many parts that resonate with you and speak to your heart.

As a mother who suffered the death of my newborn son, Christian, in 2007, I felt incredibly isolated. The deaths of babies and children were unspoken topics. No one close to us had been through something similar. There was very little support available, and if we wanted it, we had to get dressed, leave our home and drive over an hour to attend a support group meeting. In that first year, I found getting to the store for milk difficult. There was no way I was going to muster up the energy and courage to drive across town and share my innermost heartbreak with a room full of strangers.

I wish there had been a book like this back then. It would have made me realise much sooner that I was not alone, that I was not going crazy and that I was going to be okay – that the sun would shine for me again. I needed someone to tell me that my child's life had meaning and that I had the power to give him a great legacy of love. I can see this book becoming a companion for those who find themselves on this unimaginable path. It is a wonderful acknowledgement of all that we endure in our first year of grieving.

Nathalie Himmelrich has created a heart-centred community through the Grieving Parents Support Network. On a road that begins with smoke and mirrors, this book is a gift and a guiding light to all who find it. You will find your way. It might not be the path some want you to go down, but that is okay: this is not their journey. This is your loss, this is your love, this is your life. You, and you alone, get to decide how you will grow for your children from this moment forward.

May this book give you the courage and strength to live your new life with great meaning and purpose to honour the life of your child. Always know they are loved, and they still matter.

From Christian's beach with heart,
*Carly Marie Dudley*

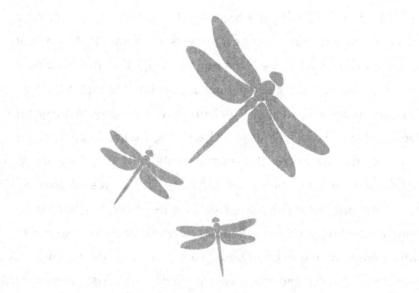

SECTION ONE

# WHEN YOUR WORLD FALLS APART

## SURVIVING A PARENT'S WORST NIGHTMARE

# LEARNING TO FLOAT

## HEATHER STROM

We knew the day our baby girl Georgia, our first child, would die. We got to choose it.

We went to bed one night knowing that the following day would be our last with our only child. We didn't get much rest, but in the morning we did as we had done for the previous forty days. We got up, got dressed and headed for the NICU for the last time. We chose the time, and when that time came, we chose a time a little later. We held Georgia as her breathing tube and IVs were removed, and we shared her final half hour of life with tears, smiles and a lot of kisses. We bathed her, held her, took pictures of her and, when the afternoon grew into evening, we wrapped her in a blanket and left her with the nurse to take her to the morgue. We walked out of the hospital the same way we'd walked in forty days prior: with empty arms.

I had prepared myself for the grief. I had grieved for her even before we knew for sure we'd have to say good-bye. I had thought that, because we knew the end was coming, I would somehow have a head start on grief and be able to resume my previous life more easily having prepared myself for life without Georgia.

What I hadn't prepared myself for was living a life *after* her; I had only thought of life without her. I had lived the first thirty years of my life *without* her, and I didn't realise that it would be so breathtakingly different than the two and a half years I've lived after Georgia left my world.

The first few days at home were a blur: funeral planning, finding a cemetery, trying to find funeral clothes that would accommodate my newly un-pregnant body and organising a barbecue for seventy-five of our friends and family that wanted to join us in Georgia's honour. They had read our updates on our social media and felt as though they knew her. They had experienced the ups and downs, anticipated doctors' opinions and cried when we cried. They wanted more than anything to try and bring some comfort to our broken hearts.

**I had grieved for her even before we knew for sure we'd have to say good-bye.**

The day after our memorial barbecue, my husband and I packed up leftovers and our bags and set out on a road trip. We drove for thirty straight hours from Minnesota to Georgia. We knew that, after breathing dry hospital air for forty days and crying until we had no tears left, before we tried to acclimatise to our new lives – our "new normal" – we had to get away.

For whatever reason, although there was no actual connection to our daughter other than her name, it felt right to be in the state of Georgia. It was as though we were surrounded by her. Even the welcoming sign as we crossed the border reminded us that, "We're glad

Georgia's on your mind": it felt like a hug.

We spent two days in Atlanta and then moved on to Daytona Beach, Florida. We stayed in a hotel right on the beach. For the next few days, I awoke to a sunrise that made me never want to leave. The salt in the air from the ocean seemed to replenish the salt I had lost in tears.

When we returned home to Minnesota, there was more blur. I went back to work. I began to learn my triggers. And I found reasons to keep breathing. I can't tell you how many times I wondered why I, of all people, was the one that had to live through this experience. Why did everyone else I knew have healthy babies while I was left with restless arms with nothing to hold? What had I done to deserve this? Those questions are still unanswered, but I am at peace with them. I don't know why I was chosen to experience such heartbreak, but I am thankful that I was given the gift to meet someone – my daughter – who would make such a profound difference in my life.

To keep my idle hands busy, I exhausted all of my creative outlets. I made a shadow box by collaging all the cards we had received for Georgia. I meshed them all: from baby shower, to first Easter, to "Get Well Soon" and "Thinking of You" to sympathy cards. I cut out each signature, message and pretty picture on each card and made them the background of my shadow box. I took the "G" off her nursery wall and put it right in the middle of the box. I added her footprints, hair bow, ultrasound picture and ID bracelet from the hospital. It is still on display in our living room and I love how it encompasses her life.

I took up sewing. I used blankets we had bought for her and those she had lain on in the hospital and made teddy bears I called "Georgia Bears". The blankets were some of the few items she had been able to use in the hospital. I kept three of the bears. I also gave one to my mom and one each to my niece and two nephews. My eldest niece, Addy, was just three when Georgia lived. Although she didn't get to meet Georgia,

Addy knows about her and expresses that she loves and misses her. It brings tears to my eyes whenever Addy mentions Georgia or includes her when telling someone about her family. Giving the bears to them brought me comfort. It allowed me to share her with them and enabled me to give them a piece of her that they could hold. I have pictures of Georgia with each print of fabric, so they can see that they were hers.

I began to share my Georgia Bear project and made bears for other people, using their loved ones' clothing. I made thirteen bears from the clothing of one woman's grandfather. She gave each of her family members a bear for Christmas, and I was able to see pictures of them hugging the bears. I did the same for the family of a close friend when her grandmother passed away. I think it gave me more comfort to give other people something tangible, something they could hold in their arms. Helping them grieve also helped me grieve.

I formed "Team Gigi" the fall after Georgia died when I came across information on a fundraiser walk to benefit foundations that research congenital heart defects. I couldn't pass up the opportunity to raise money on

> My daughter died, but she also lived, and both are equally important to acknowledge.

Georgia's behalf with the hope that our contribution, albeit small, could help bring about the breakthrough that would ensure a future where no parent has to make the decision we had to make. We have participated in three annual walks and raised several thousand dollars in her honour by selling Team Gigi shirts. I can tell you that it still catches my breath sometimes when I see someone wearing a shirt with her name on it.

When I look back at the early days of my grief, before I had managed to pick up all of the shattered pieces of my life as I knew it,

I wonder how I kept going. I wonder, in amazement of my own strength, how I managed to keep waking up in the mornings and going through the motions. I felt as though I was drowning, and all I could do was grasp at the tiny memories I had to keep me afloat. I can see now that eventually, through my creative outlets, I wasn't flailing around trying to stay above water. It was when I learned to submerge myself in Georgia's memory that I felt a weight lifted off my shoulders. My grief did not go away; I just learned to coexist with it and use it to spread her memory as far as I could. Essentially, I just learned to float. It sounds crazy, but I feel as though when I was finally able to put my shattered pieces back together, I could see more clearly, love more deeply and relate to people in emotional pain on a much deeper level than I ever had before.

I am unapologetically in love with my children, whether I hold them in my arms or carry them in my heart. They are a part of me, and I will live my life in a way that would make them proud. This is the only way I've found to help me continue on in life. Of course, I live life for *me*. I make a conscious effort to include Georgia in the life I live with my husband, family and friends, because it validates that she is mine. Family pictures, holidays, stories: she's always represented. I am who I am because of her.

My daughter died, but she also lived, and both are equally important to acknowledge.

*Heather Strom is a previously unpublished writer who uses her creative outlets as a means of recognising and navigating through her grief after the loss of her daughter Georgia Jeanne.*

# INHALING AFTER HEARING THERE IS NO HEARTBEAT

## DANIELLE RIDGWAY

The sun was shining that day. It was a beautiful spring day. Any day now, I would deliver my child whose weight was sitting more heavily than just the day before. When I got out of the car, the wind whipped through my hair. I took a deep breath as I waddled into the doctor's office. I didn't know it then, but it was the last deep, careless breath I would take for a long time.

"Danielle, you are next", spoke the technician. I was ready for the check up to begin. I was excited to see my baby dance across the screen just as he had done three days before. The ultrasound technician smiled as she squirted the gel on my belly. I joked about how much the baby was moving the night before. Today was the day the doctor was going to tell me when I was going to be induced. Everything in my life was falling in place. Then, I saw her face and heard words come out of her mouth that I will never forget.

"I'm so sorry, there's no heartbeat".

That moment, after those words reached my ears, was the longest moment in my entire life. The world came to a crashing halt as I exhaled all the air from my lungs. My skin burned. Tears pouring out of my eyes sliced their way down my cheeks. There had to be sound, since I felt the technician's hand grab mine and saw her mouth forming words. She helped me sit up, but my vision went black. My thoughts whirled aimlessly. I couldn't understand what the sentence meant or believe that she had said it to me about my baby. This couldn't be true.

## I had always promised him and myself that I would be the best mother to him that I could.

Somehow, her words were true. We rushed to the hospital only to see him still on the ultrasound three more times. Each felt like another stab in my heart. I was induced and thought it would take days for him to be born. During the short five-hour labour, I don't remember breathing. After I heard the news, I never inhaled. Even when they were counting my breaths to push, I don't think air ever reached my lungs.

The moment he was born, I felt myself inhale. This sharp breath was waiting to hear a cry that was already not promised to me. It was a breath taken in hope that all the machines had been wrong, that he was my little fighter who defied all the odds. That one breath marked the beginning of my life without my son: a life that I had never imagined or wanted to embark on. I inhaled the moment around me. He was being carried away to the room next to mine while the nurses kept checking my vitals. All I could hear was the person sadly calling the time: 4:25am is the exact moment when everything changed.

From the moment I took my last deep breath to inhaling after his birth, I didn't think I'd make it. Every moment felt like my heart was going to stop beating just like his. If it could happen to him, as he was safe in my belly, how could it not also happen to me? I felt so vulnerable and broken. How would I ever pick up the pieces of my shattered life? Was my life even salvageable? Deep down I knew that I wasn't supposed to be consumed by the despair of losing him. That's not what he would have wanted for his mom.

I had always promised him and myself that I would be the best mother to him that I could. I had not expected a silent motherhood. That thought had never crossed my mind. He was supposed to be with me every step of the way. I was going to be his biggest cheerleader, help him with his homework after school and be the person he could talk to about anything. His life and the dreams I had for him were full of positivity. There was no way I was going to let death steal all of that away. Death had already taken my son, but it would never take my memories or love.

With his silent birth came my rebirth as a loss mother who would live the rest of her life fighting to be the voice her son never got to use.

> **Death had already taken my son, but it would never take my memories or love.**

When I reflect on what I once thought of as my weakest moments, I now see the seeds I had planted. They were strength, endurance and the will to keep moving forward from the worst set of words I have ever heard. The seeds were nurtured by love and the bond I have with my son. They were buried so deep that it took a while for them to sprout. As each has grown stronger and tangled with grief, I can see the beauty that I have created. The words that once broke me have motivated me to do better. I relive that scene at least twice a day; nonetheless, I do my best to take that pain and turn it into something more manageable.

At first, I had to focus on me. I began by just taking a shower when I felt sad or setting an alarm to remind me to eat. When the pain felt like it was seeping out of me, I wrote it all down. I scribbled and screamed into each word. That guided some of the anger out and let me smile again. Yes, I could smile and laugh after the hardest and longest moments of my life. Self-care was hard to practice in those first weeks, but those small acts were absolutely crucial for me to keep moving through each day. It helped me jump into what really started healing my heart.

> Self-care was hard to practice but helped me jump into what really started healing my heart.

I knew thousands of other women had heard those dreaded words. They too remember the last carefree breath and the first harsh one that loss brings. Knowing all those amazing mothers also felt that pain motivated me to reach out and help: whether that was making someone smile at support group or talking to someone I knew was hurting. Being able to help at least one person a day, because of my son, gave me a purpose again. Helping another person made me look forward to tomorrow again, something I didn't think I would ever get back to. To this day, I combat my pain with the values I wanted to instil in my baby. Just because he's not here to learn them doesn't mean I can't live part of the life I had dreamed about. This was the purpose of my rebirth. It helped fill my heart with even more love and hope for the future.

Losing him triggered my rebirth and has allowed me to create a beautiful support circle. The moment I knew he was gone, I didn't think I could experience being a part of this world again. The world had abandoned me. The world had taken the only human connection

I had ever wanted. Then, mothers who had felt that same pain warmly welcomed me as a sister in loss. Although I wish I could give it all away to have my son back in my arms, I'm so thankful for each and every single one of them.

It all started with a deep breath walking into the doctor's office and taking my first breath after his birth. Then I could start focusing on this journey of loss and love in the best way I know possible. It's not an easy route. It demands a lot of self-care and compassion. This type of motherhood is painfully beautiful. I know no one can see the little boy that follows me. But they can see the love, the strength and my persistence to keep going on for both of us that radiates off me.

*Danielle Ridgway's life was changed forever when her son, Jensen Grey, was born sleeping. Even though Jensen was born silently, Danielle refuses to stay quiet about his life and the stigma around stillbirth. This was never the motherhood Danielle expected, but after her and Jensen's dad's lives took separate paths, she embraces being Jensen's mom with the support of family and friends.*

# I WOULDN'T HAVE IT
# ANY OTHER WAY

## CHRIS YOUNG

Watching my tiny daughter lying in the NICU, tubes keeping her fragile body alive, her twin sister resting nearby, small but healthy, I was torn between an agonising mix of hope and despair. Happiness at the beautiful birth of our twin girls was challenged by the fear that Amya Mirica would probably not survive. Her lungs, improperly developed, could not keep even her small body alive on their own, and scans soon revealed that other vital organs were also missing.

I looked on helplessly as her lungs failed, and I pleaded with the doctors for any possible solution we could try. The incessant beeping of machines and the intensity of the NICU environment were overwhelming. After two of the longest days of my life, it became clear that my precious child, with whom I had felt such close connection as she developed within the womb, could not live with the conditions with which she had been born. Prolonging her life artificially would only subject her to more discomfort and increased risk of infection and other complications.

Having to watch her die was heart-breaking. Knowing I would

never get to see her grow up, that her mother would have to bear the loss of one of her miracle twins and that her sister would now grow up without her twin by her side, I could hardly breathe. The pain felt as if a knife was slowly turned inside my body. Dreams of future events shattered. Thousands of possible moments that would never be experienced played through my head.

I wanted to be angry, but with whom? With my daughter, who had made every effort to live despite her body's inability to do so? With the doctors, who had done everything possible to save her and make her short life comfortable? With the universe, for which one tiny life in the vastness of all of space and time was merely a brief random event?

I felt that I had failed. I knew, logically, there was nothing more I could have done, but as a man and a husband it was my "job" to protect my family. I was supposed to look after my daughters, not allow one to die and then eventually have to explain to the other one why her sister wasn't there to play with her and grow up with her.

In the days that followed I moved on auto-pilot. I remember those days through a haze. It felt completely unreal, and I couldn't believe this was really happening to us, to me. A few days after we returned home, a stranger broke into our home while we were

> As a man and a husband it was my "job" to protect my family.

there and stole my wife's bag with her phone and wallet. I flew into a blind rage. I screamed with fury and ran out of the house hunting the culprit. I shudder to imagine what would have transpired had we met in those moments. Fuelled by my pain and unresolved anger, I think I could have been capable of extreme, unreasonable violence.

Life went on and required actions to be taken. I helped make funeral arrangements while also assisting in looking after our newborn daughter. I cried often. Our living daughter was a constant reminder of the child I had lost. Taking care of my wife and our new addition became a focus, something to take my mind off the grief that came over me in waves.

After a few weeks, I returned to work but found it difficult to focus. I worried about things that previously wouldn't have bothered me. I felt emotionally fragile. I lacked my usual confidence that things would work out well. I checked on Ananda Mae regularly at night to see if she was still breathing and worried constantly that something might happen to her. When my daughter developed an earache I was terrified that it was something serious, and we ended up taking a late-night trip to the hospital to check on her.

Looking back, I realise I threw myself into doing anything I could to be a support. If I had "failed" to protect Amya, I would do my best to be a support to my wife and our wonderful, precious Ananda Mae. I would like to be able to say that some specific thing made a difference in my journey, that there was a magic bullet that helped me through the darkest times and led me to the light. In truth, the only real healing agent has been time and a willingness to share openly about what has happened. I have no faith to lean on; no one process, technique, workshop or person particularly helped me survive the darkest days and emerge from them, like a butterfly, transformed and whole again.

At the beginning, I did attend some group sessions at the hospital. It helped to hear other parents share their experiences and know that I wasn't alone. I read several books, which helped me feel that my experience, my emotions and my challenges were like those of other parents who had experienced the death of a child. Perhaps the most useful thing I did was to be open and share what had happened with those around me. The people where I worked were amazingly supportive, giving me time off when I needed it, willing and open to talking about what had happened and how I was feeling about it.

I didn't feel a need to undertake other forms of therapy or actively participate in child-loss communities, even though I believe these have great merit and can help many parents through this experience. Instead, for me it has been the process of grieving day after day and learning that the loss of Amya Mirica is part of who I am. It does not define me though. I don't label myself as a "child loss dad". I do not

> I miss her every single day, and I wouldn't have it any other way.

expend energy in creating a role for myself in that context. I am a father of two daughters, one growing up each day and the other held within my heart. When I am asked how many children I have, I answer honestly that I have two, but that one is no longer living.

My wife, Nathalie Himmelrich, has written a book on the grief process that parents go through (Grieving Parents: Surviving Loss as a Couple). In proofreading her book, I realised that the single biggest lesson for me was that we all grieve differently. I think it is fair to say men tend to grieve differently than women. For me, the grief journey has been largely internalised. To an outsider, it may not have looked like I was grieving at all, but I can assure you the pain was just as real. During this period, I found myself repetitively listening to the Limp Bizkit song, "Behind Blue Eyes", and thinking how well this applied to me. I felt that the pain that resided behind my own blue eyes was not known by outsiders. My love and grief for Amya Mirica had become a sadness and an anger that had no direction or place to go.

And so, I continued to live my life and move forward doing the things that needed to be done. Gradually, the grief transformed. I began to laugh more often and cry less frequently. In my mind, I see a great mountain that may take many years to ascend, and the only thing I can do is to climb one day at a time, moving forward and upward.

In our neighbourhood there are several families with twins, and there are twins attending Ananda Mae's Kindergarten class. It's painful to see them walking together, wishing Ananda Mae had her own sister to walk with her. Sometimes Ananda Mae asks why she can't have her sister to play with or cries that Amya Mirica isn't here with her. There is nothing I can do to "make it better". Indeed, it is a truth that life is not always fair and that sadness needs to be experienced. I hold her and let my own tears run, for I have no answer as to why and her pain reminds me of my own.

Never do I want the sadness to go away. It no longer cripples me. Instead, it serves as a reminder, an honouring, of the daughter I will never get to know: Ananda Mae's "angel" sister. Every new event is a reminder that she is missing: every birthday, the first day of school and first time riding a bike. I wonder about the person Amya Mirica would have been, how she would have been similar to her sister and in what ways she would have been her own unique self.

I miss her every single day, and I wouldn't have it any other way.

*An entrepreneur and consultant, Chris Young is also an avid fan of Science Fiction and Fantasy films and novels. He is the father of twin girls Ananda Mae and Amya Mirica. While still hurting from the death of Amya Mirica two days after she was born due to Potters syndrome, Chris continues to look forward to new challenges and loves spending time with his wife Nathalie and daughter Ananda Mae.*

grief is
a reflection
of love

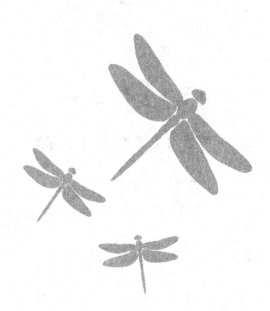

# SECTION TWO

# YOU ARE NOT ALONE

## FINDING YOUR COMMUNITY OF SUPPORT

# FROM SINGLE MOM TO SINGLE BEREAVED MOM

## JULIA SORKO

From day one, I thought being a single mom would be my biggest life challenge. Luisa's dad and I separated before I even knew I was pregnant. During my pregnancy, he changed his mind a few times when it came to his role as a father. We were not together anymore; a baby had not been the plan. At first, he wanted me to have an abortion when he learned about my pregnancy. He then came around and said he would play an active role as her father. During the last weeks of my pregnancy, he entirely retreated from me again, and I couldn't guess whether he would participate in her life. My family wanted to support me, but they all lived several hundred kilometres away in Austria while I was living in Germany. These were the parameters for starting my own little family. However, I was happy, excited and looked forward to life with my baby.

I had always wanted a family. I accepted that this apparently meant life as a single mom. Then Luisa died unexpectedly nine days after being born, and suddenly I became a single, bereaved mom.

I suffered two huge losses at once. I had secretly hoped during pregnancy that our sweet baby girl would bring her father and me back together once she was here. That did not happen. After her birth and sudden death, I hoped our tremendous pain of losing her would do so. It didn't. Perhaps we would at least grieve together as her parents. That also did not happen. His actions piled pain on top of pain. To this day, I still do not understand his actions.

Contact between us declined to zero over the months following her death. As the pregnancy progressed, I had sensed there was no space in his life for Luisa. Now that Luisa was dead, there was no reason to make space for her. My family grieved heavily. I found comfort knowing this but could not shake the emptiness I felt of Luisa having only one parent grieving her.

Then, to remove any doubt, Luisa's dad declared our ways would separate for good. We have all had our hearts broken. It is a part of life. But this man is my baby's dad. This heartbreak is more intense. Three years later, I am still not ready and trustful enough for a new partnership.

The time since Luisa died went by so quickly on the one hand, but on the other hand, it took me a long time to somehow piece my life back together. The first year was like living in a thick fog. The state of shock ebbed away after

> **This was not a nightmare from which I would awake.**

several months. I realised what had happened. This was not a nightmare from which I would awake. This was my new reality. Intense pain and desperation set in. I felt the pain physically. It terrified me. What if it stayed like this? I felt so helpless. My life was meaningless without her. I had no idea what to do with myself.

My heart and my body were all set to be a mom 24/7. In my head, I had this permanent thought of, "I was supposed to take care 24/7 for my baby. Everything I do now is just wrong, a forced alternative".

A huge challenge was my loneliness. I lived alone. I spent many hours alone, crying with no one there to give me a hug or talk to me. I felt lonely even when I was with others. I believed I didn't belong anywhere, and when I tried to interact I felt misunderstood. It was a difficult time.

## I felt lonely even when I was with others.

I could have returned to my parents' home after Luisa died, but I couldn't do it. I know it was difficult for them, especially my mom, not being able to check on me in person and having to rely on phone calls and messages. But I was paralysed from the grief and shock and clung to the only stable thing I had left: a town I knew, my apartment, my friends. Any more change was unthinkable at that time.

Also, I knew that at some point I would have to return to work. With my state of mind, I could in no way go through a relocation and job search. In addition, I had started weekly psychotherapy sessions a month after Luisa died, because I suffered from depression. My therapy continued for two years. I needed therapy, maybe because of my special situation as I was also single, the double loss of baby and partner and the consequences from that. Now in year three after Luisa died, I manage my ups and downs on my own, without a therapist. I take pride in being able to do so.

The friendships I made within the loss community were and are an incredible source. Shortly after Luisa was born, I attended a special postnatal course called *Leere Wiege* (Empty Cradle) for bereaved moms. The combination of professional support from my therapist as well as newly-formed friendships from the Empty Cradle group and the incomparable understanding I received from other bereaved moms became my most important supports to survive my loss and keep going. They also kept me in Frankfurt.

Almost two years after Luisa's death, and with the help of therapy, I finally found the strength to quit my job in Frankfurt and leave that city behind in order to move back to my home country, Austria. I took a six-month sabbatical to regain strength, recover and start anew. I made a wise decision.

"Do you have kids; want kids?" are questions that are so hard to answer. Future plans, pregnancy and babies have become huge, sensitive topics and triggers ever since Luisa died. I was thirty-three when she was born. In that same year, two of my best friends became moms. Also, my sister-in-law was due with a girl four months after me. I stopped counting the healthy babies born around me ever since my girl died. Why did it only happen to me that my healthy, full-term baby died from a fatal cord accident during birth in a hospital, a place I chose for us to be safe?

Also within my Empty Cradle group, the first moms became pregnant with their rainbow babies. As happy as I was for them, this deep emptiness within me grew deeper. I longed to have a baby, a sibling for my girl, to make my arms and my heart full. I am aware of challenges coming with pregnancy after loss but I also see the hope, meaning and a new sense of happiness it brings my bereaved mom friends who have their rainbow babies in their arms. I was and am single, and so there was no real option for getting pregnant. Perhaps sperm donation, but I am still not ready for that, for various reasons: emotional issues, legal concerns and simply lack of strength to go through another pregnancy alone.

I want a partner, a dad for my child or children and a real family. Something that seemed so natural to achieve in life somehow became

> My life was meaningless without her. I had no idea what to do with myself.

an uncertainty. This combination of wanting a baby, being lonely and having been deeply disappointed by my baby's dad was difficult to process. It did force me to give my grief for Luisa space and time and not rush things by getting pregnant too soon, which would have been likely for me had I had the chance. I had to slow down. Process. Cry. Create a different space in my life for Luisa than the one I had anticipated. Raise awareness for pregnancy and infant loss. I engaged in all sorts of healing modes. I continuously dealt with my new self.

Luisa's death changed my perspectives on life, family, friendship and countless other aspects. Her death generated enormous struggles for me and my closest circle of family and friends. I am convinced for some, not only me, there will be a lifelong scar and effect. We live a new normal where the simplest, most common things can be painful reminders of losing Luisa. I have learned to live without her physically in my life.

> My daughter died, but I didn't die with her. I survived and life goes on.

I adapted. Everyday life is okay now. Holidays or family events remain difficult. I will always speak of Luisa proudly. By being open about my story, I hope to create awareness for others that it is possible to survive.

I don't know what life has planned for me in the future, but I try to actively create my future every day. As I write these thoughts, three years have passed since I lost my baby girl. Things have changed; many things have become better. There have been many firsts since Luisa died: spontaneous laughter, singing, being funny, enjoying things, feeling fine, holding other people's babies. During the first year and most of the second year, I didn't believe that doing those things was even possible. Life was sad, empty, dull – unbearable.

There were times in which I didn't want to go on. I did everything I could. I tried healing of all sorts: yoga, acupuncture, osteopathy, homeopathy, massage, Emotional Freedom Technique, journaling and sharing on social media. Honestly, it was a lot of work. Getting better didn't happen overnight, and I was often too impatient with myself. However, I persevered and healing came in increments. Now I have many more stable days than bad ones. My story will continue, and Luisa is a big part of it because she will always be my baby girl. I will always love her the way a parent loves a child who is no longer present.

Luisa died, but I didn't die with her. I survived and life goes on.

*Julia Sorko became a single bereaved mom when her daughter Luisa died unexpectedly shortly after birth. Surviving this loss without Luisa's father by her side complicated this journey, but she did not give up. In fact, supporting other moms going through similar situations gives her meaning and strength.*

# EXPECTING NO MORE

## CHRISTINE STABLER

Her nursery was lavender. Ballerinas danced across the sheets of her newly delivered crib. An ivory, faux fur bunting hung neatly from a hook on her wall. Life was perfect. I was newly married, and at age thirty-six, I was ready to bring our beautiful baby girl into this world.

To my surprise, I became pregnant quickly. Aside from the normal bouts of nausea during the first trimester, and the achy back as my belly grew, the pregnancy was smooth sailing. Before I knew it, I was thirty-seven weeks pregnant. My hospital bag was packed. We were counting down the days.

It was a chilly Veteran's Day in Washington, DC. My husband and I both had the day off. My husband's cousin was in town from the Midwest, so we met up for an early dinner. My belly felt huge, and I was swollen. I couldn't even button my coat and my feet were stuffed into the only pair of shoes that would fit.

Our little girl was a mover. She was constantly on the go. I sat on our bed and waited for the cute little kicks and punches as I did every night… only I didn't feel anything. I had a glass of cold water and a Hershey's Kiss, but still nothing. I called my doctor. She told me to head to the hospital, where staff would check me out, but she was not worried that anything was wrong.

Our drive to the hospital was almost leisurely. The staff was expecting us, so we were put into a room with an ultrasound almost immediately. A nurse used a Doppler to find our little girl's heartbeat. I was annoyed that she couldn't find a heartbeat, and it wasn't until she hooked me up to the ultrasound that I said, "You can't find her heartbeat, can you?" Two doctors came in to confirm that there was no heartbeat. Our perfect world was now upside down as we sat in the dark room sobbing.

Sofia Noelle Stabler was stillborn two days later on November 13 at 5:01am. She was a perfect six pounds, five ounces, with a full head of the darkest hair. She looked so peaceful. I wanted so badly for her to wake up, for her chest to start moving, for Sofia to open her eyes. I held her lifeless body though the irony of it was that I too felt lifeless. I wanted to leave the hospital. I was up and dressed in no time; my legs still wobbly from the epidural. Little did I know that the hardest part would be leaving without my baby. My empty arms ached. Something felt so unnatural about leaving her there. It was not fair.

Both my family and my husband's family flew in to be with us immediately. No one really knew what to do or say. I wanted to keep busy. I thought I would be able to take my mind off the fact that our baby died, though it was impossible. My body was sore. I ached all over. But I pushed through in order to avoid just sitting at home crying. Seeing pregnant woman and newborn babies was torture.

I wished neither the women nor the babies any harm. I hurt so deeply. Just days ago, I was expecting, and we were planning for our beautiful little girl's arrival.

After our families left, I found it almost unbearable to go out in public alone. I tried, but I felt like the world was buzzing around me and I was frozen in my grief. Thanksgiving was just around the corner. I remember standing in Whole Foods feeling so overwhelmed that I had to leave and go home. Well-intentioned neighbours in our building would congratulate me on having my baby because they would see my now deflated stomach. I would look like a deer in the headlights as I tried to explain what had happened. I thought they looked at me as if I did something to cause my baby's death, though I now know how irrational my thinking was at the time.

Thanksgiving came and went. Christmas was absolutely brutal, as was New Year's Eve. What was usually my favourite time of year became a time that I wanted to pass as quickly as possible. I was on a leave of absence from work. I could not bear the thought of going back to a place where the last time I had gone I was pregnant.

**My experience has allowed me to meet some of the most incredibly strong and inspiring people.**

I sat in Sofia's nursery every night. The room was so peaceful and beautiful. I read a book where a mom wrote letters to her stillborn daughter. I started to write letters to Sofia each night. I did that for a while, and it felt good. I found a therapist in our area who specialised in grief and pregnancy loss.

My husband and I went two or three times, though we were not as open as I think we needed to be.

As the weeks passed I decided to make a promise to myself. Although she was not here with me, I wanted my daughter to be proud of me. I got out of bed every day, showered, put on make-up, got dressed and faced the world. I found a local support group called MISShare. It met on the first Thursday of every month. I did not expect to get much out of it and sort of had a preconceived notion that it would be a "woe is me" kind of group. I wanted to give it a chance though, so I went.

I realised I wasn't alone. My feelings were not crazy.

The group was completely opposite of what I expected. The two women who ran the group had both experienced loss. Most of the women there had experienced late term losses. One, whom I connected with almost immediately, had delivered two successive stillborn babies. Everyone had an opportunity to introduce themselves and share their stories. I realised I wasn't alone. My feelings were not crazy. Others shared the same feelings. I got advice on everything from how to deal with work, to coming up with a mantra for those awkward elevator encounters when people congratulated me on having a baby. The group built me up. The more I went, the more momentum I gained to face each day. I was much gentler on myself. I realised that Sofia's death was not my fault – that I did everything right. I also learned that I was still a mom and no one could take that from me.

Between meetings I connected with Carly, the woman who had suffered consecutive stillbirths. She was and is the strongest person

I know. We shared pictures of our babies and stories. We cringed together when pregnant women or babies came into the coffee shop where we would sit for hours and talk. There was honestly no better therapy. We understood each other like no one else could.

Carly and I became each other's cheerleaders. When I had an appointment with a high-risk Obstetrician-Gynaecologist to discuss future pregnancies, Carly was as eager as I was to find out what the doctor said. When my husband and I went back to visit family and no one even mentioned our loss, she understood. Like me, she had similar worries, concerns and feelings. The biggest of those worries was if we would ever be able to have other children. Fortunately, she and I became pregnant again at the same time. The most ironic and special part of it all was that her daughter was born on November 13, a year to the day Sofia had been born.

## I don't even think I had ever heard of a stillbirth until it happened to me.

In my worst dreams, I could never have imagined suffering the loss of a baby. I don't even think I had ever heard of a stillbirth until it happened to me. Though heart-breaking, my experience has allowed me to meet some of the most incredibly strong and inspiring people: people I may never have had the opportunity to meet. They were real people just like me. They had experienced similar tragedy and their feelings mirrored mine. These people picked me up in my darkest hour. They held my hand and led me through my grief. I am eternally grateful for their guidance and love.

Three years have passed, and I always tell people that your

grief never goes away. It just gets more "palatable". I am now at a point where I can help navigate others through their grief because of what I have learned. Ex-coworkers, friends of friends and others who have had the misfortune of suffering a loss have reached out to me for guidance. My hope is that I am able to lead them and build them up as well as those who did the same for me.

Max James Stabler was born on December 2 at 12:18pm.

*Christine Stabler's life and priorities changed drastically when her first child, Sofia Noelle, was stillborn at thirty-seven weeks. As a result, she left her job with the federal government. She spent time working with the Kelly Ryan Foundation, a non-profit organisation which helps pay burial expenses for those who have suffered the loss of a pregnancy or an infant. Christine, her husband Nick and their two-year-old son live in Connecticut, USA.*

# SECTION THREE

# A DIFFERENT YOU

## RECOGNISING THE PERSON IN THE MIRROR

# CHOOSING TO SEE LIFE IN COLOUR

## ANDREA VURDEA

Whenever I think about my old self, I see a beautiful, smiley, innocent and carefree young woman: a woman who knows no pain or sorrow; a woman whose heart shines bright with love and laughter; a woman who believes in happy endings. I only know that woman through the eyes of my husband. That woman is a stranger to me for I only got a glimpse of her the night she left holding my daughter's hand, the night our baby girl came silently into this world, the night I was reborn.

I often close my eyes and see that woman and Francesca running around in poppy fields under the warm summer sun. I see her holding my beautiful little girl as she reads her a goodnight story. I see them laughing and giggling as they build sand castles by the sea. If there's one person I would trust to raise my daughter, it would be her.

I'm not saying that I am the opposite of that woman, but the night she left I was irrevocably changed. I am now older, wiser, broken-hearted and sometimes bitter, but I am also a mother whose broken heart is filled with love and that is something that no one can take away from me.

I am not who I used to be, but that does not mean I am less; it simply means I am different. Sometimes different can be good; you just have to accept the change and strive to do good with what you are given.

This is exactly what all of us bereaved parents are doing: the best with what we are given.

I remember when I started walking this grief journey I was tormented by all the "whys" and "what ifs", but as time went on I learned to let go of them and fill the space with love and kindness.

Grief is such a unique experience for each of us. It's like a fingerprint. No one can really tell you when things will get better or easier to bear. What I can tell you is that if you are patient with your new self, if you allow yourself to feel all the things you need to feel and if you are kind to your shattered heart, things will get easier. In the time that has passed since we said good-bye to our daughter, I have learned that death does not define us and death cannot take away the most precious thing we have, which is love.

> I am not who I used to be, but that does not mean I am less; it simply means I am different.

Grief is just the aftermath of love, and though at times you may feel as if it will take the breath away from you, I can assure you it will not. Love can be transformed into anything that you choose. I chose to transform love into beauty and kindness and share them with the world just as our daughter would have done.

My old self was never much of an artist, but grief-stricken as I was, I found myself unable to speak of the pain that was crushing my soul, so I started writing about it. My blog helped a lot in the first few weeks after Francesca died. I felt that it was the only safe place where I could express what I was truly feeling without being judged. The first posts were filled with shock, dismay, anger, bitterness and hatred, but gradually I noticed that the emotions began to change, and love took over just as I had hoped it would.

The night our daughter came into this world I was reborn into darkness and darkness I wanted to become. Black was the only colour I could find while searching for the pieces of my broken heart, yet I felt myself desperately craving light. I craved colour. I craved love.

Along the way, I began using stress-relief colouring books. They turned into my safe haven. My husband bought the first one three days after our daughter passed away and gave it to me asking only one thing of me: whenever I felt the need to cry, I would close the book and reopen it only when I felt ready to go on. This helped immensely in creating a buffer between my broken heart and my shocked brain. I honestly think it was one of the only things that kept me sane in the first few weeks. I coloured for hours on end; some days I would colour all day, even while I was having lunch or dinner.

And so, though I had never been the artistic type, I decided to give this new me a chance to survive, a chance to learn to live again, a chance to discover beauty and a chance to see life in all the colours this world has to offer. A piece of paper, three paintbrushes and a cheap set of watercolours were the things that saved me from the darkness. And so my journey began.

Painting and drawing took up most of my free time in the months after Francesca's death. Painting and drawing helped me discover who I had become and brought beauty over a loss that seemed unbearable. Every time I picked up my brushes, I felt as if I was painting with love, not with watercolours. I painted her name over and over again, each time trying to make it look a little prettier than before. My pain was my art teacher. I let it take me wherever it needed in order to make something good come out of my journey.

Some days I painted flowers and other days Francesca's smile filled up my pages. No matter how my heart felt that day, my feelings were colourful, and I was grateful for that because it meant I was alive. Don't get me wrong, I know not all colours are happy colours, but I am glad to have found them all. I now know that no matter what they represent, be it love, hate, jealousy, bitterness rawness or just plain beauty, colours make this life worth living, just as feelings keep our hearts beating.

My first few attempts at drawing and painting after the loss of our daughter were not something I would call works of art. I had so much I wanted to express through my drawings and a clear vision of what they should look like. Yet, the end product seemed like something a kindergartner would have drawn. I remember feeling upset about it, but I also remember my husband's voice cheering me on, telling me to keep painting what I was feeling, and so it began.

I began drawing mandalas to represent my world and to express my hope for the future. Every mandala piece began with my drawing the perfect circle on a piece of paper and then drawing her, the most beautiful ballerina, in the middle of it. She was, after all, the centre of my world. Next, I filled the rest of the circle with whatever I felt that day: things I was unable to talk about but felt the need to express. Looking back on the mandalas, I can clearly see a gradual transformation of the soul and of my feelings. The first ones represented the darkness I found myself in, but as time went on, light and hope crawled in a little more with every piece. In the beginning, I drew stories of caged birds and trees of life with no life left in them, stories of seasons to pass and never-ending winters. As love emerged out of the darkness, I started drawing nightingales flying free in the starry sky. I drew blossomed cherry trees and poppy fields. I drew crimson skies and sunrises I never thought I'd want to see again. I began drawing life, and these were the things that brought me back to it, to life.

Life is a gift that our daughter got to enjoy for a very short time.

Yet, she managed to fill our lives with hope, love, colour and many memories. We will cherish these things for the rest of our lives. These are the best gifts she could have given us.

Francesca left her footprints in the sands of time as she did in my heart, and I will not leave this place without making sure her kindness makes a difference in the world. Every time my brushes strike over a paper, I will let love tell her story, our story, and let her colours shine bright as they make this world a better place. Every word I write on our journey will speak of undying and unwavering love. Every time my heart touches another's, I will know it's her grace that made it happen.

Her grace is forever embedded in my soul – just as your child's grace is eternally bound to yours. We have the power to tell their story and our story through the things we do. You might not think of yourself as the artistic type; I didn't. But at the time I needed it most, this was the only way I was able to speak of things that were unspoken, the only way to set myself free of the pain and replace it with hope.

I know the challenges you are facing might seem unbearable, and the path you are going on is not the one you planned on walking. I know you feel alone in the darkness that surrounds you, but if you choose to let love lead the way for you, I promise one day you will be able to see life in colour.

*Andrea Vurdea is a wedding photographer and bereaved mother who has found healing while discovering art. After the loss of her daughter, Andrea has found purpose in helping others grieve and heal while expressing their feelings through art. Her current goal in life is to spread love and kindness in memory of her daughter Francesca.*

# THE STRENGTH OUR BABIES GAVE US

## ALANNA SALTER

I was thirty-nine weeks and two days into a perfect pregnancy with my first baby when I found out that her heart had suddenly stopped beating. In that moment, in the cramped little scan room, with a stranger's hand on my leg and the three words "I'm so sorry", everything changed forever. Shock was followed by disbelief. Healthy babies do not die just days before their due date. All I could think was, "This can't be happening, because bad things don't happen to me".

That this was my first thought gives some clue as to the charmed life I had lived to date. I had worked hard and achieved everything I had put my mind to. I had fallen in love with a wonderful man and gotten married. Together we had overcome some initial fertility difficulties to conceive our most wanted daughter Isobel. Nothing catastrophic had ever rocked my life, and I had never had to face losing anyone I loved.

In an instant, I lost my beautiful baby around whom I had been rebuilding my life and my heart for nine months. The world in which I thought I lived was decimated. My core beliefs were shattered.

In the days and weeks that followed my birthing of Isobel and the precious time I spent with her, I began to notice all the ways in which I had changed. I felt so alien to myself, an entity unknown and ever changing, who could not be relied on to react in a predictable way to any circumstance.

Triggers to grief and traumatic memories surrounded me. Leaving the house, my unwilling hyper-vigilance to pregnancy and babies ensured that I saw both everywhere I went. Smiling parents pushing prams made my heart race. Little bundles, especially those in pink, made me feel nauseous. Women rubbing prominent bumps, so content in their naive belief that they would bring their baby home, made me want to scream. I hated that I had become someone whose heart was hurt by happy families. Staying at home was easier, but even there, reminders were inescapable.

I reminded myself that if I could get through labour knowing my darling daughter was gone, there was nothing I couldn't do.

Innocuous comedies on television would do a flashback to a character losing a baby, and songs on the radio about lost love triggered my heartache for my little girl. Social media channels were filled with friends and their children, including my antenatal group and their babies. Those babies were all around the age that Isobel should be. In order to escape further upset, I had to avoid an infinite number of things. Life closed in.

Meanwhile, anxiety (the emotion I'd always dismissed as so silly and irrational) took root. If this could happen to Isobel, if I could lose her, then no one was safe. I sat at home waiting for the next person to die, planning funerals for everyone I loved. This small, closed-in life began to feel overwhelming and hopeless.

Even though I felt life was now pointless, I never wanted anyone to say that Isobel ruined my life. I knew that this small, scared shell of a life was not the legacy I wanted for my daughter; it wasn't the impact I wanted her to have on the world. I knew I had to live boldly for a little girl that never got that chance to live for herself. I didn't want to just survive; I wanted to thrive. As terrifying as it was, I knew that this meant facing triggers, confronting fears and coping with all the emotions that would wash over me.

Having worked with emotional difficulties in my career, I had seen how avoidance only perpetuates difficulties. Avoidance of going out and engaging in pleasurable activities leads to isolation and depression. Avoiding feared situations maintains anxiety disorders. Avoiding trauma triggers fuels ongoing post-traumatic stress (PTSD) symptoms.[1] Translating this theory into action, however, was extremely difficult because my motivation and energy levels were so low.

I elected to start small:

- I watched a few minutes of my previously favourite programme about teenage mothers and their babies;
- I ventured out to the cafe around the corner;
- I walked along the river that I had anticipated pushing my pram down;
- I browsed social media and "liked" a picture of my friend with her daughter.

I discovered that the anticipation of doing something was mostly, if not always, worse than actually doing it. So many times, when things seemed too difficult, I would think of Isobel and tell

---

1    Salkovskis PM. The Importance of Behaviour in the Maintenance of Anxiety and Panic: A Cognitive Account. Behavioural Psychotherapy. Cambridge University Press; 1991;19(1):6–19.

myself that I was doing it for her. I reminded myself that if I could get through labour knowing my darling daughter was gone, there was nothing I couldn't do. Nothing I had to tackle would be harder than turning away, knowing I would never ever see her face again, as her little coffin was closed.

> ## Nothing I had to tackle would be harder than turning away as her little coffin was closed.

And indeed, nothing ever was. I would come in from a walk feeling a little more energised, leave coffee with a friend feeling a little bit lighter, reflect on my day and feel proud of myself that I had worked so hard to re-engage with life even in these worst of circumstances. At a time when I was hugely blaming myself for what happened to Isobel, these little nuggets of achievement were crucial in slowly rebuilding my confidence.

Often I had to summon reinforcements to help me achieve a goal. Going back to the yoga studio where I had practiced prior to my pregnancy and then attended for pregnancy yoga was hugely emotional. I asked a supportive friend to attend my first class with me. We arrived early to let the teacher know what had happened to Isobel before other people started to arrive. I took a space close to the door in case I had to leave. I cried all through the opening meditation. I continued to cry through much of the class that followed. But I got through that class and kept returning until it didn't feel so difficult anymore.

Soon there were opportunities to confront bigger challenges. I was offered appointments with a Clinical Psychologist, either in the maternity hospital where I had birthed Isobel or at an alternate location. Knowing that I hoped to have another pregnancy in future, I decided to return to the maternity hospital on my own terms. Driving to the appointment and then sitting in the maternity waiting room were two of the hardest things I have ever willingly opted to do.

Memories flooded my mind. My sadness was overwhelming. The physical impact of my thoughts and emotions made me want to run back to my car. However, I knew the psychology appointment could help me and it would, over time, get easier to be there. So I took some deep breaths, focused on sensing the seat beneath me with my feet firmly planted on the floor and stayed.

Every time I faced challenges like this and came through them, I felt the tiniest bit stronger. My confidence grew as I realised I could still live, even with this hole in my heart.

One thing I continued to struggle with was recognising when I needed to confront something and when I could opt out in order to protect my heart. I had to remind myself that avoidance was not always a terrible thing, and there were certain situations from which it would be wise to withdraw. The balance of knowing when to push myself and when to protect myself was one I had to work out as I went along.

> My confidence grew as I realised I could still live, even with this hole in my heart.

I learned to find compromises. When my close friend had a new baby, I decided I would go see them both, but that I wasn't ready to purchase a baby present. I brought her some groceries instead. I also let her know in advance that I didn't feel ready to hold her baby. I found discussing what I was and wasn't comfortable with prior to arriving in situations to be really important.

I could better ensure that something wasn't pushed on me in the moment that I would later regret.

I won't pretend that my strategy of "avoiding avoidance" always worked, or that there weren't days when I stayed in bed, eating chocolate and feeling supremely sorry for myself. I think those days were needed too at times! I got tired and overwhelmed much more easily than I used to.

I was exceptionally lucky in that I did become pregnant again within the first year of losing Isobel. At that point, I was so glad I had pushed myself to face difficult situations. I had practiced facing triggers and built some confidence in my ability to cope with the painful emotions and anxiety those triggers evoked.

> Life is unspeakably cruel and hard at times, it is also wonderful and beautiful, and we have to accept both the pain and the joy.

Pregnancy after loss was a whole new world of challenges, which I decided to face in the same spirit of proactive coping. I had to manage so much fear while trying to be thankful for the new life growing inside me and believing we would bring this baby home.

I created weekly routines of exercise and socialising to keep occupied. I planned day trips, massages, afternoon teas and nights away interspersed through the months so there was always a mini-goal, something to look forward to. Time passed very slowly, but it did pass, and our wonderful son Theo arrived screaming just prior to his big sister's first anniversary.

Now I'm a mother to one baby here on earth. I want my son

to learn that although life is unspeakably cruel and hard at times, it is also wonderful and beautiful, and we have to accept both the pain and the joy. I want Theo to see from us, his parents, that even though we lose people we love and it feels like the world has ended, we can learn to live again. I want to show him that we best honour our loved ones by living fully and wholeheartedly. That is the legacy I want for Isobel.

Living after the loss of your child requires more strength than I could ever have imagined, but we as bereaved parents have infinite strength: the strength our babies gave us.

*Alanna Salter and her husband, Simon, are proud parents of Isobel Olivia Salter, born asleep, and their rainbow baby Theo, born a year later. Together they offer therapeutic retreats and psychology workshops for bereaved parents in Northern Ireland.*

# SECTION FOUR

# LOSS OF SELF

## LIVING WITH THE
## MENTAL AFTERMATH

# LIVING AFTER
# MY SON'S HOMICIDE

## KATJA FABER

The magnitude of what happened to us as a family – to me as a mother – is immeasurable, the consequences incalculable.

The entire universe and the ones adjoining ours, and the ones beyond, are not large enough to contain the depth of grief now, indeed ever. Agony paralyses thought. Sorrow defeats any attempt at fortitude. Exhaustion renders me immobile. Despair fills my days and nights. My senses are overwhelmed. The anguish grinds on, wears me down. Agony rasps against my heart. I burn with pain and am driven crazy with thoughts of loss, of what he went through, of not being there to protect him, not being able to hold him as he died.

My twenty-three-year-old son was brutally killed by someone he considered to be a friend. His death has changed me. I am more fearful than I used to be. I care less about the fate of the planet. Most disconcerting is feeling numb when I see the aftermath of bombings elsewhere in the world. If your finger tips are burnt, you lose the sense of touch. So must it be with the heart. Almost two years into my mourning and with the homicide trial still ahead of us, I continue to struggle to come to terms with the new normal.

Yet there are aspects to this life-changing event that have altered who I am for the better. I no longer agonise about what life is about; I now know it's about living with grace and love and gentleness. I no longer fear death. I let the future unfold without attempting to plan or foresee every last detail. What will be, will be. I admit I am hardened in some ways, but in others, I am more relaxed and forgiving. It's as if I aged 1,000 years the night Alex died, and that wisdom has grounded me beyond my imagination. I am exhausted to the point of collapse whilst at the same time I savour every second of precious life granted me because I get to share it with my loved ones.

During the first year after Alex's death, I felt suspended in illimitable grief. Quite simply, my soul was broken. I existed, nothing more. There was no respite from the relentless, grating torment that my darling Alex was never coming home.

And yet, two years on, there is a light. It is dim: so faint that at times I wonder whether it is there at all. A warmth is beginning to spread

> And yet, two years on, there is a light.

through my veins. My days are imbued with soft colour, laughter and gratefulness. It is this last one, above all, that has led me away from the abyss. As the suffocating pain of grief began to recede, I saw with utmost clarity how extraordinarily lucky I was to feel this unending agony. The torment was a measure of my love for my child. Once I truly understood that unending grief and everlasting love were two sides of the same coin, I was able to let go of anguish. My healing began.

Because of the forthcoming trial, I am bound to silence, unable to write freely about the events surrounding my son's death in the early hours of a dark, snowy December morning. I can, however, write from first-hand experience of coming to terms with my new reality, the post-loss me and the holder of an unwanted label: mother-of-a-murdered child. I can also talk about finding the strength to channel my rage and incomprehension in order to fight for justice for my son. And in so doing, I show my still-living children that no matter what their circumstance, whatever happens to them, I will be their champion, their defender, their protector, their mother – even in death.

A brutally violent death generates extremely difficult problems for the victim's family. Clinical evidence shows that following a homicidal death, most family members are at risk of developing sustained psychological reactions such as post-traumatic stress disorder (PTSD)[2] because nothing has prepared any of them for this devastating event. The violence inflicted on one family member is felt by all; it is an attack on the very essence of what makes up a family. Any sense of safety and security is annihilated. A victim's family members may suffer from PTSD, nightmares and feelings of guilt, fear and anger. It is also common to experience a loss of self and loss of control, due to the violent nature of the crime.[2] These are brought on by stress, anxiety, numbness, self-blame, guilt and fear to name but a few.

We, the parents of the dead child, are cast in a very difficult and delicate role. Not only are we forced to deal with sudden loss; additionally, as a family we face public scrutiny and the dissection of our loved one's life during the police enquiry and the criminal legal process that follows. At a time when our entire world is shattered into a thousand pieces and we seek gentleness and privacy, we are thrown

---

2    van Wijk A, van Leiden I, Ferwerda H. Murder and the Long-Term Impact on Co-Victims: A Qualitative, Longitudinal Study. International Review of Victimology. Sage Publications Ltd; 2017;23(2):145-57.

into the public arena and, in my case, expected to show fortitude and the presence of mind to deal with prosecutors, police investigations, forensic evidence, autopsy reports, court hearings and huge legal costs.

Because bereavement caused by homicide is possibly the most extreme form of loss experienced, the victim's family may be ushered to the therapist's room posthaste in the hope that specialist counselling will alleviate suffering. And so it was in our case. Psychotherapists were found for my children, whilst I was put in touch with a lady who assured me she had experience in treating people bereaved by homicide. For us, it was a waste of time. We knew what caused our pain – grief over Alex's death combined with horror at how he had been killed.

**I did not need analysis; I needed comfort.**

I did not need analysis; I needed comfort. I did not want medication to dull the pain. I elected to leave therapy.

Instead, I turned to the Internet, and there I found connection: online forums for family members of homicide victims and Facebook groups dealing with child loss. It really helped being able to chat and comment, to have proof that I was not alone. We supported each other, looked at each other's photos of our loved ones, spoke of our anger, shared our despair and acknowledged our sorrow.

In those online conversations with strangers, I found guidance and counselling. They helped me gain an understanding of what we, as a family, were going through. They provided a context in which to place my experience and gauge how far I had come in even being able to chat online.

I took tiny, imperceptible steps but steps all the same.

Insomnia was another constant, so I read. Books arrived in the post via Amazon, on my Kindle and through kind friends. I soaked up every book on grief, child loss, partner loss and any loss before moving onto philosophy, religion, self-inquiry, criminal procedure and criminal law. I watched YouTube videos, listened to TED talks and tuned into counselling radio shows and podcasts so long as they had something to do with death. Whatever gave me insight into the loss of my son and my response to it was consumed in a desperate bid to gain a better understanding of what had happened to me and, most importantly, how to travel this not-chosen path.

Nature became my companion. I walked in the woods, and I spent time planting trees, picking fruit and growing vegetables. The creation of life and its slow decay were testament to the passing of time. The seasons had never mattered more, to see the snow melt, buds in spring, summer storms and falling leaves. I felt the world spinning around the sun and saw how my hair turned grey and my still-living children grew taller.

**My life as I understood it has ended; the new me has had to find a way of living a new life.**

Too worn out and fearful of able-bodied, whole-hearted, full-of-life strangers, I avoided crowded, public spaces where the uninjured rushed about unaware that my life lay shattered at my feet. Knowing that I needed to do some exercise for the sake of my mental and physical health, I enrolled in aqua gym classes at the local hospital. Safe among others whose brokenness was visible, I was able to weep as I swooshed and jogged in the warmth of the physio pool. We were all united in our desire for recovery. Whilst the loss of a child is not the same as a new titanium hip operation or the after effects of a stroke, there were similarities in how we approached what lay ahead: fortitude, good humour and tenacity being among the many traits I could mention. The benefits of this weekly baptism were near miraculous: I felt I was back in the womb, my movement in water helping me heal on some primordial, unconscious level. I am not a swimmer, and water has always frightened me, but truly, this experience helped immeasurably in that first year. Even now, I continue with classes and I would not for the world stop, for I have much to learn and oceans of grief yet to explore.

My life as I understood it and as I lived it has ended; the new me has had to find a way of living a new life. It is hard, very hard, but I sense that it may be possible. I am forever indebted to those who have been at my side throughout this ordeal, to friends and family whose loyalty, generosity and love have supported me. And all those who have written, phoned or sent messages to share stories about Alex or simply ask how we are. I do not know what the future holds, but I do know that whatever lies ahead, the love I feel for all my children will give me the strength to keep going. It is a very long journey and I see no end, but then there doesn't need to be. One step at a time.

*Katja Faber is a single mother of three children. Her oldest son, Alex, was brutally killed at age twenty-three. Trained as a lawyer and journalist, she left her profession to be a full-time mother, later becoming an avocado farmer once her children were in their teens. She has worked tirelessly for justice for her dead son as a means of channelling her grief and helping her living children come to terms with their brother's violent death.*

# "YOU HAVE POST-TRAUMATIC STRESS DISORDER"

## EMILY MCENTIRE

I almost laughed aloud when I heard the counsellor say those words to me. Thoughts raced through my mind: I'm not a soldier, a victim of violence or assault. What is she talking about?

As I headed home, I thought about what she had said. The symptoms fit: inability to sleep, reliving the moments over and over, insecurity, paranoia, a sense of impending doom, irritability, no thoughts of the future and, of course, my greatest shame: forgetting I was pregnant.

And that was it: my greatest shame, the one thing I was too embarrassed to say aloud. I finally admitted it to my husband while unable to look at him. I constantly forgot that I was pregnant. Not in a fleeting moment of absent-mindedness, but constantly. I spent my days bumping my stomach into things and wondering why it was so big, feeling my baby move and thinking I had bad gas cramps and finding myself unable to sleep at night because of thoughts and dreams of my three miscarriages. I felt crazy, out of control, as if there were something wrong with me. Seriously, who forgets they are pregnant?

This wasn't my first pregnancy. I had two healthy children. But this pregnancy was different. The entire nine months were filled with fear, anxiety, endless tears, forgetting I was pregnant and an inability to bond with my baby. Images of my three previous miscarriages clouded my vision.

Nine years ago, I miscarried the first time and had been too ashamed to tell anyone. The miscarriage took three days to complete. I carried on with life as usual, not even allowing myself to stop and grieve. Two years ago, I miscarried twins at eleven weeks. At the doctor's office, the on-call doctor was oblivious to what was happening and did not listen to me when I tried to tell her what was going on. She was doing an examination and pressed down on my lower abdomen. I watched in horror as what was left of my twin sons fell out onto the floor and were scooped up in tissue paper and thrown in the garbage without a word to me. That memory still haunts me. A month before getting pregnant with JoyAnna, our rainbow baby, I had been in my bathroom holding our daughter in my hands after miscarrying her. The experience of those losses left me with holes in my heart and made me question my value and ability as a mother. They are memories I was unable to share with anyone.

> Those losses left me with holes in my heart and made me question my value and ability as a mother.

The day finally came. I was welcoming labour, looking forward to this nightmare of a pregnancy to finally end. But I was in for another terrible round of post-traumatic stress disorder (PTSD). My labour with our rainbow baby was unlike either of my other two, full-term deliveries. I was at home in early labour for twenty-eight hours before leaving for the hospital and giving birth eight hours later. During that entire time, I became caught between two conflicting worlds: one of complete terror, the other being perfect peace. I needed to feel every aspect of this labour and delivery, to convince myself it was real, so I went without any medication. My contractions felt exactly like each miscarriage. I struggled to keep my mind focused on the fact I was in labour and having a live, full-term baby, as my mind began to shut down and forget I was pregnant. When waves of contractions came, I panicked and then forcibly reminded myself I was in labour. My

**In that room full of strangers, I found peace.**

body was doing its job. After thirty-six hours of reliving the worst moments in my life, I was anticipating the fulfilment of a promise. I have never experienced terror on that level and was shocked to still be feeling God's perfect peace at the same time. That time was a crucible for me, a testing ground and a turning point.

After taking our sweet baby girl home, we were thrilled. Our daughter and son (then six and three) were excited to finally have a baby to hold. They had lived through the aftermath of two miscarriages and understood what it was to be missing part of our family. Two months after JoyAnna's birth, I found myself struggling to cope, to find emotional stability and to bond with her.

I joined a grief support group at a local church. Over the following thirteen weeks, I discovered healing in a way that I never knew existed. Finally accepting the words that a counsellor had told me seven months earlier about having PTSD gave me the ability to address the problem and begin the healing process.

I spent the first five weeks of the thirteen-week course unable to say a word. I could only sit there and cry. Amazingly though, in that room full of strangers, I found peace. A peace that, even in the midst of chaos and horrible grief, told me I was not alone. Not once in my crazy, forgetful nine-month pregnancy had I ever felt an emotion or feeling that any other woman had not felt before. My PTSD symptoms were normal. Not normal for everyone, but having PTSD did not make me crazy. If anything, it showed I had loved deeply, and deep love is nothing to be ashamed of. As I allowed myself to grieve for all four of my babies now in heaven, I found I was able to love myself, my family and my perfect baby girl in a deeper and complete way. Embracing the waves of grief, flashbacks, sleepless nights and anxiety allowed me to be able to talk myself through each step and reassure myself that even though things were not okay now, they would be someday.

Recently my sister-in-law went with me to a gravel pit with a box of dishes. She stood beside me and helped as we hurled the dishes one by one at a pile of sharp rocks. Watching the dishes shatter and break into a million pieces, I felt the walls around my heart crumble. I talked to her about some of the deep pain and fears I had been

> The dark season is no longer what defines me. It shaped who I am now, but it does not define me.

hiding and ashamed of for years. I am so thankful I was able to open up. Being able to talk about my feelings and the "crazy" that I thought myself to be was the best way to bring healing to those broken parts. I finally felt it was okay to be sad about my losses.

JoyAnna is seventeen months old now. I love her more than

I thought was possible, and I love all our kids that way. I still have good days and bad days, but definitely more good ones now. I drew a picture of a tree with four birds flying out into the sky. The four birds flying away represent our four babies who have gone to heaven. I know what it is to love and lose what you love. To have the thing I'd prayed for years to hold, only to have it taken away before I was ready to let go.

I believe God is good. I believe God loves us in ways we cannot understand. While I do not always understand the way things happen, I am thankful God gave me those babies to love and carry, even if it was for just a short time. I know I will see them again. I know we will finally be a complete family in heaven. I know at the end of the day, my faith in God, my hope in an eternity together and the knowledge that God is good are what keep my heart beating.

I am finally able to dream about the future. I can picture my kids and imagine those years down the road when they are older and have their own children. I am not consumed by the "what ifs" of life. I trust God that no matter what happens, I will be okay. I have walked through a dark season and walked through it more than once. The dark season is no longer what defines me. It shaped who I am now, but it does not define me. I have hope for the future and it is full of love and life!

*Emily McEntire is a mom to seven children, three on earth and four in heaven. She resides in Seattle, Washington where she enjoys homeschooling and cooking, as well as being outdoors for hikes and time near the ocean. Emily is passionate about life, love and family.*

# BROKEN PARTS AND ALL

## ALICE R. GRAHAM

I have lost people in my life before: my father, when I was six years old; my friend, when I was nineteen. We all thought we were invincible: aunts, grandparents and distant relatives. I work in Aged Care and deal with losing palliative residents and their grieving families quite often. Looking back, I suppose I was at a point where I thought I knew and understood loss, grief and death. However, there is nothing to prepare anyone in any way for dealing with the loss of a child.

I lost my son, Charlie, on July 1st. I was diagnosed with HELLP syndrome, a severe and life-threatening pregnancy complication. HELLP stands for haemolysis (red blood cells needed to carry oxygen around the body break down); elevated liver enzymes (liver function decreases and harmful enzymes are released into the body); low platelet count (blood doesn't clot). It is often thought of as a severe form of pre-eclampsia. I was very sick and the only way to save my life was for Charlie to be born at twenty-three weeks. Our local hospital was not equipped to deal with my condition and had no NICU facilities for such a premature baby, so I was transferred to the city three hours away. We were hopeful that in the city hospital, the medical team could stabilise my condition and keep me pregnant as long as possible, giving Charlie a better chance.

My partner agreed to come up the following day after organising care for our

**Anxiety was a new and unwelcome part of my life.**

other two children and letting everyone know what was happening. Unfortunately, during the three-hour ambulance ride my condition deteriorated. By the time we reached the hospital I was told Charlie would have to be born immediately or we would both lose our lives. My little boy lived for forty short minutes. He died before I woke up. I spent two weeks in the hospital. Because of the emotional intensity of the events leading to Charlie's birth and death, I would later be diagnosed with post-traumatic stress disorder (PTSD) combined with severe anxiety.

I have always been "The Boss" in our family. I made the decisions. We lived on my income. I made plans and organised my partner and our children. I oversaw everything; delegated chores and remembered who had what, when and where. I was happy with this, until I couldn't do it anymore. I came home from hospital physically weak and emotionally battered. I struggled to think, to speak, even to remember things.

Words had always come easily to me. Now they got tangled in my head. I called things by the wrong name or was not able to get words out at all. I was broken: physically, mentally and emotionally. I hadn't only lost my baby; I had lost myself as well.

I sat on the couch and cried. I lay in bed and cried. I didn't sleep.

I didn't eat. Whenever I shut my eyes, I was back in the operating room, miles from my home and my people. I could feel Charlie's vigorous kicks. Amidst the wonderful sense of life, I succumbed again to the horrifying knowledge that he wouldn't survive. Without having any voice in the matter, Charlie gave his life for mine. I begged the doctors and nurses to not make me do it. Flashbacks kept happening: vivid, horrible memories. In the shower. In the car. In the street. A smell, a noise, someone's voice. Anything could set it off. I felt like my head was in a vacuum. I carried immense guilt about letting Charlie down, about letting my other children down by being so useless. I wanted to die.

Anxiety was a new and unwelcome part of my life. I went from having control over everything to having no control. One day, I went to the store in need of milk. I walked in and knew everyone was talking about me: "There's the lady whose baby died". I was convinced everyone was looking at me. The walls closed in on me. I forgot what I came for. I couldn't breathe. I couldn't cry. After an experience like this, I'd go home where I could cry and feel like the worst person in the world. I would lay down on the couch, a safe haven, and sob. I felt like I was losing my mind. I wanted to die. I couldn't understand why I was still here. What purpose was served by my going through this unique form of hell?

At first, the grief was overwhelming and constant. I could hardly go a minute without losing it. Then there would be a brief period of time where I would be halfway between awake and asleep in the morning. My mind would be clear, and for a few seconds I felt like the former me. Not sad, not broken, just waking up like every other day. And then, all at once, everything would crash down on me. After about a month, one morning I decided to get up and eat with my children before school.

They still needed me, and they were here. I dragged my miserable self out to the kitchen and my five-year-old daughter saw me and called out, "Yay! Mummy!!" It was nothing really. She was just happy to see me, but to me it felt like she was cheering me on, celebrating the massive victory I'd just had: getting out of bed. And that was the start of it.

I don't remember consciously deciding to get back up and live, but this is the closest to it. Little by little, I let my family back in. I never consciously shut them out, but my mind had turned its back on everyone in my life. My grief was selfish. I couldn't see that I wasn't the only one that was hurting.

**She helped me realise that it was okay for me to not be okay.**

Opening the doors to my family was the start. We talked. We talked about Charlie and how sad we were that he wasn't here. We looked at his pictures the nurses had taken while I was asleep. We cried. We cried as a family. Around this time, I began to see a counsellor to help with PTSD and anxiety. She helped me set small challenges to find myself again, to find the new me. She helped me realise that it was okay for me to not be okay, that it was okay to hand over control of the everyday things to someone else. It was okay for me to cry, to be angry and to feel ripped off. She gave me a place to scream if I needed. And she listened without judgement.

I started to walk. Living near the ocean, I would walk along the beach. No one could see me cry or wonder why I was throwing rocks into the waves and yelling abuse at the sky. I had a place to go where there was no judgement. I stopped crying on the couch.

I read, and I wrote. I wrote to Charlie. I wrote angry letters and sad letters. I wrote down our story. I read about other parents. I read about their beautiful children whom they had lost. I read about their heartache. I started to feel like I wasn't alone. I took comfort in the fact there were other people who, unfortunately, knew what it felt like. They understood.

Sadly, not long after Charlie died, one of my dear friends, who had been a rock for me and my family, lost her beautiful fourteen-year-old son. From the moment she called me, I knew I was needed. I knew why I couldn't just give up and die. My life had a purpose. My friend and I stumbled along this journey of loss together, taking turns picking each other up, finding reasons to keep going when everything felt hopeless and dark.

We decided that if we could make it through the first twelve months together, we could make it through anything. We gave ourselves things to look forward to: a concert, a show or a holiday. We made deals with ourselves, never looking too far into the future, because honestly, a future without our children still

> I have learned to allow myself to be sad, to cry, to be angry and to wonder what could have been.

feels too big. We talk about them, we remember them and we constantly wish they were here with us. We spend special days remembering them: their birthdays, the anniversaries of their death, Mother's Day and Christmas. We never forget them: they are a constant missing presence everywhere we go, in everything we do. They always will be.

I am blessed with beautiful friends in my life, near and far away, who call, message or email every day just to check in: my family, my brother and his wonderful partner, my children, my parents, people who are empathetic to what I have been through and what I am still going through. I have learned to allow myself to be sad, to cry, to be angry and to wonder what could have been.

I keep a journal for Charlie, as I do for my other children, where I write notes and keep pictures for him. I live my life as best I can. I find comfort in helping others, talking and writing about my experience, about Charlie's short life and mine. I have lost friends and gained others.

I have learned to put myself first. While that may seem selfish to some, I don't mind. I try to surround myself with people who impact my life in positive ways, who help build me up. I choose to be with people who support and carry me when I need it.

> I choose to be with people who support and carry me when I need it.

I talk about my little one, my son Charlie, because he was here and he did matter. I encourage my children to talk about him. Charlie will always be their brother, always loved and missed in our family. I celebrate his birthday. I light candles for him, and I have a memorial fountain in our garden that I can see from my bedroom. I have his handprint tattooed on my wrist. I will hold his hand until the day I die, which it turns out, I actually hope is a long way away.

There is no easy road through the first twelve months, or in fact through the rest of my life. I have accepted that some days I won't want to get up. Some days I will be jealous of all the mums that get to keep their babies, and yes, there will be moments when I will be angry and bitter. I will be heartbroken and sad for all the moments I have lost with my little one. There will be people who think I should "get over it". There will be people who don't understand. And that's okay. There will also be good days, even great days, when I will laugh without guilt. There will be people who love and accept me, broken parts and all. I will enjoy the rest of my life to honour my son, to live what he has lost, what he gave to save me. He will live in me until my last breath.

Alice R. Graham is a mother of three and works as a nurse in Aged Care. After losing her third child, Charlie, at twenty-three weeks, she decided to write about her experiences to help her through her grief, and hopefully to support and inspire others dealing with loss.

SECTION FIVE

# CARING FOR YOUR WHOLE PERSON

## PHYSICAL AND SPIRITUAL SELF-CARE

# EXPECTING RAINBOWS

## KEEM SCHULTZ-FARES

G et down, you'll break your neck!" How many times have we, as parents, called out those words to our children? I only wish I had seen Karina climb up the goalpost frame. My children and I had arrived at my brother's home in Mexico the previous night to spend a school break with his family. My husband stayed behind to finish some work and was to join us later in the week. The five cousins were excited to spend time together and the four younger children, including my nine-year-old son Mark, looked up to Karina as the oldest and the natural leader.

The morning after we arrived, all five kids went on a little after-breakfast hike up the crest of a small hill. My sister-in-law and I watched from the kitchen window. "Take care of the little kids!" I told Karina as they set off. We saw her carrying her two-year-old cousin David part of the way while the others raced along. She was always their guide, their protector, their example.

Later, in the afternoon, we all decided to take a walk. We set off,

Karina corralling the kids up ahead while the adults leisurely trailed behind chatting. We stopped at a playground and allowed the kids to swing and slide for a few carefree moments. Mid-conversation, as we continued across the soccer field beside the playground, my brother suddenly called, "Watch out!" I turned to see Karina falling toward the earth.

She had climbed a metal goalpost frame and proceeded to do gymnastics manoeuvres she had done countless times on the bars at her gym back home. The frame was not anchored, and the momentum of her movement and weight of her body caused the goalpost to tip and crash to the ground. I ran across the grassy field and, in what felt like a superhuman moment of strength, I hoisted the metal frame off my daughter's crumpled form. She had landed as if she were starting a somersault, but the back of her neck was flush to the ground. Her arms were limp beside her bent knees, and her head was tucked under her chest. I knew immediately that her neck was broken.

My sister-in-law herded the four younger children away as my brother ran, shouting for help. I was alone with Karina in the grassy field for what felt like an eternity before others began to approach. A few people, all strangers, knelt by my side and joined me in fervent, whispered prayer. I could see the shock in their faces. Others fell to their knees at the perimeter of the field. It took emergency services nearly two hours to reach our remote location, and all they could do was pronounce Karina dead on arrival. I gave them permission to cover her with a white sheet. That's what they're supposed to do, right? But then I removed it from her face. Her beautiful face with its short, but dark, thick eyelashes and her still-round baby cheeks. My fearless girl.

We had celebrated her twelfth birthday only five days earlier at an indoor obstacle and ropes course. Karina had attempted every challenge. She always sought after faster and higher. Now she lay still while wild rabbits frolicked in the shrubs and birds swooped low overhead. My athlete, my gymnast, my precious girl. Gone in the blink of an eye. How was it even possible?

She left us quickly, but everything else moved in slow motion or ground to a halt. I forced my numb legs to walk into a restroom to wash Karina's blood off my hands before I went to tell Mark that the ambulance had arrived but the crew couldn't do anything to help his sister. His sweet little boy's mind raced furiously to try to comprehend what I was saying; I could not yet say the word *dead*. Three hours after the initial fall, when the coroner finally left, my dad arrived. He didn't know. He offered to pray.

> There is no way to prepare for the sudden death of a healthy, active and vivacious twelve-year-old.

"It's too late, they took her", was all I could say.

It was dark outside when I finally spoke to my husband. He had been contacted to come, but knew no specifics and was making the three-hour drive across an international border alone. Again, I couldn't bring myself say the word dead.

"She's gone", I told him.

"No, no, no..." was all he could respond.

There is no way to prepare for the sudden death of a healthy, active and vivacious twelve-year-old. My husband and I had planned responsibly for our own inevitable deaths, purchasing life insurance, drawing up a will and trust and discussing end of life matters. We had also discussed what might happen when our parents died. However, we never considered that we might lose one of our healthy children. In the months that followed, the thought that continuously echoed in my head and worked its way out my lips in a silent scream was, "It's not possible". The sheer, crude horror of the situation still overshadows everything.

I have only shared the rage of my heart and voice with a couple of individuals. My sister-in-law has become my strongest supporter and advocate, always ready to listen or do what I needed most, even when I didn't know what I needed. My husband has been a rock. Though racked with grief himself, he holds me for hours while I allow the sobs and horrible sounds to run their course.

The sobbing didn't happen in the first days after Karina's death. In the immediate aftermath, many things required our attention. In the midst of making arrangements, notifying friends and hosting arriving family members, we focused heavily on Mark. We tended to his gentle heart and dealt with the anger directed at God, expressed through hot tears and the questions for which we had no answers. We reiterated our trust and hope in heaven, and relied heavily on our personal faith to accept what we could not understand. We have continued to cling to that faith as time passes. The morning between Karina's memorial service and her burial, we awoke to an incredibly clear, complete rainbow in the canyon behind our home. So close, we could nearly touch it. We immediately recognised this beautiful sign as confirmation of God's promise of hope.

Each awful death date (I prefer the term "crapiversary") is difficult for me. Every Wednesday. Every eighteenth of the month. Those dates loom over me, and sometimes I make it through them only to crumble in and anguish and emotional exhaustion a day or two later. Even more difficult for me is that few people take note of these days; causing me to feel more alone in my grief.

One friend wrote, "Why does the sun even shine today with grief so heavy?" Writing those words again here, even now, brings me to tears. My heart cries, "Yes! Why? How?" Life quickly returns to its regular patterns for everyone around us, and we are left with the cruellest truth: life and living go on despite our suffering.

Music does wonders to soothe my broken heart. Songs that eloquently communicate depth of emotion are a godsend. A playlist by Kristen Gilles called "For Grieving in Hope, Funerals", and collaborative playlists by *Still Standing Magazine* and *Grieving Parents Support Network*, all on Spotify, have been lifelines. Not being much of a writer myself, I have scoured the internet desperately for blog posts and articles that give expression to my grief. I have found very few accounts that deal with losing an adolescent child to a sudden, accidental death. Still, child loss and general grief communities have much to offer. I have found that sharing songs, articles, images and quotes on the Celebrating Karina Facebook group gives me an outlet for expression and helps educate those around me on the realities of grief and child loss.

> I no longer recognise myself or the life I'm living.

After Karina's death, I consciously gave myself thirteen months of complete grace. If I didn't want to get out of bed, I allowed myself the comfort of my covers. When I felt the need to participate in an event like the Kindness Project or Wave of Light, I did so, even if my husband and son didn't see the point. I mostly didn't answer phone calls, because I found chit-chat pointless and demoralising. I didn't invite my mom to stay with me, because I couldn't bring myself to care for anyone beyond my immediate nuclear family. I don't think I even cooked a meal or styled my hair for a year. I also avoided social interactions, especially group settings where I had to meet new people. I still give myself grace to do these things or not do things. A lot of it was and is simply about survival. Much of my day revolves around the needs and activities of my son, but even now, I am cautious about scheduling too much in a day or a week. I find I need a day of complete rest every few days.

Brutal honesty is how I best handle my grief. When people ask how I'm doing, I don't say, "I'm fine". When the question comes up, I say I have two children. I tell people when comments aren't helpful, and I suggest alternatives to standard expressions of condolences. Much of this is done through my postings to the Facebook group. Being honest includes being honest with myself and others about what I do or do not need. I've learned to ask friends for help with things like picking up items at the grocery store, because the thought of seeing Karina's favourite cereal on the shelf causes me anxiety, or going with me to a grieving mothers support group, because I'm too vulnerable to go alone.

> Being honest includes being honest with myself and others about what I do or do not need.

I've allowed friendships to shift and change. Some of my most supportive friends are not persons I was close to before Karina's death. In part, this is because I need physical closeness more than long-distance emails or calls. In some cases, friends have been uncomfortable with or raised concerns about my honest expressions of grief. Instead of trying to explain something that cannot be understood by someone who has not experienced it, I have at times chosen to move on. For me, it's all about survival. I do what I need to survive in the moment.

I left and continue to leave online and in-person support groups that are not helpful to me. Online communities that focus too heavily on loss and desperation drag me into a pit of despair. Other groups that centre on the loss of a spouse, parent, pregnancy or infant, or that deal with death due to suicide, overdose or childhood illness have simply not met my needs. Even groups catering to mothers who have lost children haven't always been the right fit for my experience or personal beliefs. I allow myself to move on. I survive.

I no longer recognise myself or the life I'm living. Am I the mother of a vivacious, talented, caring teenage girl? How do I guide my son through life as an "only" child, when he is not? How can I be a support and helpmate to my husband, Karina's "Papi", when I can barely help myself? I have no answers. I simply survive one moment, one day, one week, one month, one year... and then do it again. Maybe someday I'll have survived enough to live, and perhaps even thrive. In the midst of my own darkness, I can trust and hope that a rainbow may appear. I anticipate the moment when light breaks through the heaviest clouds and splashes vibrant colours across the sky in a grand gesture of promise and of hope. The colours may dissolve quickly, but then I will wait for the next one to come. One stormy day at a time, I am expecting rainbows.

*Keem Schultz-Fares struggles to rediscover herself after the accidental death of her twelve-year-old daughter, Karina. She finds joy in her son, Mark, and strength in her faith in God. Keem and her husband established Karina's Joy Foundation to perpetuate Karina's joyful spirit and giving nature through youth scholarships and acts of kindness.*

# LEARNING TO BREATHE AGAIN

## TARA RIGG

I opened my eyes one morning after a deep sleep and immediately felt a shift in my world. I knew something had changed. My intuition told me that something was wrong. I lay in bed waiting for my baby boy to give me a kick or a jab so I would know he was okay. When it didn't come, I got up, ate some yogurt, drank some juice and waited. When a kick or jab still didn't come, panic gripped my chest, and I raced to my doctor's office.

First, a nurse tried to find his heartbeat with a monitor. For a moment, she thought she heard it, but I told her, "I think that's my heart you hear beating rapidly". She searched for a few more minutes before she decided to take me into the nearby ultrasound room. After a very brief moment looking at the screen, she left the room and asked a doctor to come in. The doctor confirmed Beau had passed away at some point during the night. The next day, after a long induction, my husband and I held our baby boy in our arms for the first and the last time. We left the hospital empty handed, but we were carrying much.

In the days that followed, my milk came in fiercely then faded away. My body went through all the normal things a body goes through after giving birth, including post-partum bleeding and cramping, which slowly subsided over the course of a few weeks. I was familiar with the post-delivery process, having had three babies before.

# The littlest things set me off. Sometimes I broke down in tears.

But this time my baby wasn't there for me to hold. After six weeks, it was time to return to exercising and getting my body back in shape. At least that was what society was telling me. In my mind, I knew exercise would be a healthy choice. Yet in my heart, I dreaded it.

I attended a few Mommy Boot Camp classes. I left feeling upset, because all I could think about was how much baby weight I had to lose, but I had no baby. I thought about explaining my situation to the class' overly intense instructor, but I couldn't put the words together. I wanted to tell her that I used to be in decent shape; however, now I couldn't run very far or do many push-ups because I had recently delivered my fourth child. I wanted to tell her that breastfeeding had always helped me recover after my previous deliveries; this time, though, I couldn't breastfeed. It was just too much. I stopped going.

Life continued around me. Our three daughters still needed their mom. Staying home all day with a four-year-old and two-year old twins, while trying to grieve and to process my son's death was draining and incredibly difficult. The littlest things set me off. If one of the twins refused to take her nap, or if my four-year-old whined about what was for dinner, I either stormed off or started yelling. Sometimes I broke down in tears. This happened several times a day, every day. The happy, gentle mother they once had was gone, and I knew they missed her as much as I did.

My husband carefully suggested trying to exercise again. He felt that it would help with my depression and anxiety, as well as give me something positive to do. Exercise and being active in general was helping him with his grief tremendously. A part of me worried exercise would make my baby weight go away, and deep down I didn't want it to. That weight was the last piece of Beau's physical existence that I could hold onto. Another part of me didn't want to face healthy, strong people at the gym who had no idea of the nightmare I was in. I resisted doing any sort of exercising for months.

Finally, after continued encouragement from my husband, and mainly just to escape the house for a short respite, I dragged myself to our local recreation centre for an evening yoga class. I had taken a few yoga classes in the past, mostly worrying about whether I was doing the poses right while wondering if I looked as ridiculous as I felt. I knew I needed to get out of the house, and I had begun to feel the need to move my body in some way.

> The happy, gentle mother they once had was gone, and I knew they missed her as much as I did.

I walked in and avoided all eye contact as I quietly borrowed a mat and unrolled it in the very back corner of the room. I sat down and closed my eyes. I didn't want to engage with anyone there, including the instructor. Thankfully, she didn't approach me and class began. The instructor led us through a few gentle stretches, then into a few poses. The room was very quiet. That felt good to my ears. I focused on the instructor's voice. She had a soothing way of explaining what to do next, without being too technical.

She spoke about breathing over and over. I had heard yoga instructors talk about breathing before, but I always believed that breathing was a side activity that was optional. I believed yoga was mostly about doing some good stretching and perhaps a little strength training. This time I listened closely. I took the first real, true, deep breath since losing Beau. In that moment, clear words came into my mind:

"I'm breathing".

"I'm alive".

Those simple words struck me. For the first time in many weeks, I realised Beau was gone. But I was still alive.

I was alive.

I had forgotten.

These words followed in my mind: "And the girls are still alive. They are breathing, too".

Tears flowed down my face as I realised that my girls were still with me, still thriving, growing, learning and breathing in my presence. Those precious daughters needed their mama to be breathing and living, along with them.

The class continued and the instructor's words came to my ears with clarity and grace. A glimmer of hope ignited within me when I heard the instructor tell us, "You're grounded. You are strong, like a warrior", as she demonstrated the poses.

"Open your hearts to the sky. Breathe life into your cores", she told us. Her words inspired me. I claimed them. I believed them.

She continued, "Yoga is all about finding calm in difficult situations". The exact words I needed to hear at the exact time I needed them most.

That yoga class was the first real step I took on my healing journey. It was the moment I began finding a balance between grief and joy. I think of that balance each time I hold a difficult pose or try a new one. Often, I fall. However, I have learned to try again and each time I try, I am able to hold my balance a little longer. This is true in yoga poses and in life in general as a grieving parent.

Each time I unroll my mat in a new class is a new opportunity for me to heal, to grow, to learn. Physically, yoga slowly melted my baby weight away, while strengthening my weak heart. By making my body stronger, I was stronger in facing my grief.

I have been to many classes with different instructors and have learned something new from each one. Some have demonstrated different poses that they say are particularly helpful for those who are grieving. Others speak of finding peace as you struggle with balance.

## I was breathing. I was alive. I had forgotten.

Whenever my anxiety increases, waves of grief intensify or I need to reconnect with my son, I turn to yoga. I find classes online, at studios, at recreation centres and in gyms. Most have one-time drop-in fees. Many are low-cost or free. Finding the right instructors and the right environment have been key. As the months went on in my first year of grief, I had moments where I needed to set time aside to be with my thoughts and with my pain. I wanted to focus on my son and my loss. Yoga has been that time for me: time which I set aside from my busy days to simply *be*. I breathe deeply. I see that breath coursing through my body – my present, alive body.

Through yoga, I learned how to breathe effectively when I experience moments of deep pain. Breathing is such a simple human act but an act that is so difficult when I feel I am drowning. Breathing to simple counts, in and out, in and out, helps me survive the moment until the waves recede.

Yoga taught me to find calm in the midst of the most difficult situation of my life. Most importantly, yoga taught me how to breathe again.

*Tara Rigg gratefully breathes in the mountain air surrounding her home in Bozeman, Montana, USA. She lives with her high school sweetheart husband and their three young daughters. She frequently writes about grief and has had several essays published on Scary Mommy, Parent.co and Still Standing Magazine.*

# CROWNS, THE BLESSINGS OF A LITTLE LIFE

## DAVID COOKSEY

My son, Nathaniel, was stillborn. At Nathaniel's funeral, the pastor shared an image that struck me. The pastor said Nathaniel would have many crowns. From a faith perspective, a crown signifies great achievement, good things attributed to one's life. That suggests that Nathaniel's life would have significance and impact. How could this be? Nathaniel was born still. Nathaniel would not affect the world for good with his own hands, from his own acts or words.

I realised the good had to come from other hands: those of his father, mother, sister, grandparents, any whose life Nathaniel had touched during the pregnancy. I will never fully realise on this earth what all his crowns may be, but I will remain vigilant for what I see, what I might experience.

I faced going back to work. My wife Amanda would be at home without Nathaniel, who should have been there. Amanda was also recovering from her emergency C-section. Adding to her challenge – and mine – was dealing with our three-year-old Abigail, who was as lovable and difficult as any three-year-old should be.

I could no longer be present through the day to comfort them. I could not help Amanda by putting Abigail down for a nap. What three-year-old ever wants to take a nap?

I had to work, not just grieve. I had to face the normal day with work, but this was a radically changed normal, not the one I had lived before Nathaniel's birthdate. This journey I had never even considered, a journey without Nathaniel. Even though I knew it was all very real, I kept hoping I would awaken from a horribly bad dream. But it wasn't a dream; it was indeed our new normal.

Like others before me, I asked, "Why me? Why should my family be dealt this lot in life?"

Even before we left the hospital, I decided to tell my co-workers – the people I saw each day and would pass in the halls at work – about the loss of Nathaniel. I work in a large facility and walk by many colleagues in the halls each day. I had shared my excitement as a father expecting a son. I tearfully composed an email that would go out to a large distribution list. That was the best choice for me so I wouldn't be forced to tell again and again the circumstances in which I found myself with this loss.

When I returned to work, a dozen or so co-workers sought me out to express words of condolence and comfort. A few shared that they too had suffered a loss. Most of the time the exchanges were good, even helpful. At least once, I was not prepared at all for the conversation. I had just finished my workday and was headed to my car. Someone whom I didn't recognise approached me.

"Are you David?" he asked.

"Yes", I answered.

"I am so sorry for your loss", this stranger said.

I was unprepared for this and stammered, "It's okay. We have been blessed in many ways from Nathaniel's loss".

It felt so insincere to leave it at that; there was no time to explain what I meant since we were each walking a short distance to our cars.

I had been back to work maybe a week. Everything was still raw. This man had tried to express his sorrow to me and it felt like I blew it off with a trite saying that I knew he either didn't understand or didn't believe.

On the way home, I decided I would try to prepare better for situations like that. I thought through several responses depending on how familiar I was with the person and the length of the conversation I would have. With the team I worked most closely, I let them know days when I felt particularly sad. I kept my boss informed about those times when I might not be able to participate in a work conversation or meeting. I would use those moments to pray and be alone with God.

My wife and I agreed we would not hide nor ignore the loss of Nathaniel. He had been a part of our lives and would continue to be in memory. In our house, we have hung pictures of us with Nathaniel. On my desk at work, I have framed pictures and a flipbook of pictures.

> I'll admit that, sometimes I was happier to answer the question about my wife's grieving than my own grief.

I find comfort in looking at these pictures, even through tears. Missing Nathaniel is an everyday occurrence.

One of the most challenging things to deal with was the perceived notion that I was not grieving, that only my wife was grieving the loss of our son. No one said this directly, but it was implied in a question I got quite often: "How is your wife doing?"

I expected a follow up question: "And how are you doing?" That question was seldom asked. I am glad my co-workers and colleagues were concerned about Amanda. I admit, sometimes I was happier to answer the question about my wife's grieving than my own grief. However, I needed acknowledgement of my grief as well.

I managed this with a few friends by answering how we were doing. Most caught on and started asking about my grief and well-being. A few friends I had to tell outright that they could ask me the same question. Perhaps as men, we are better able to handle how women feel. Sometimes I wrestle to even determine how I feel. To deal with my feelings or the feelings of another man is, for some reason, more uncomfortable for men than dealing with the feelings of a woman. I needed a few friends who would hear me out so I could verbalise the sense of loss and deal with my grief.

Recognising what triggered moments of grief and learning how to handle those emotions at work was very important. I found that almost once a week I would have a more challenging day with grief than others.

It took a few weeks for me to recognise that Thursday had become the hardest day for me: at work, at home, even just getting out of bed in the morning. Then I remembered that Nathaniel was born still on Thursday.

Once I realised that, I took more time for myself on Thursdays. I found a song I played all the way to work that would let me grieve. "I Will Carry You" by Selah spoke to me. I told my boss and co-workers about my Thursday struggle. They were okay with my arriving late to work as I finished crying in my car in the parking lot.

My wife recognised that every month would bring a wave of grief as well. We instituted what our daughter calls Baby Brother Day. Each month, as a family, we do something special to remember Nathaniel. It can be as simple as a dessert or going out to dinner or as involved as engaging in a full day activity as time and schedules permit. Having something to look forward to once a month to celebrate Nathaniel is helpful.

A new tradition came about during the beginning of the Christmas season. We decided, on one of the monthly Nathaniel remembrance days, to decorate a tree in our yard, which we had planted in Nathaniel's memory. We get lights and ornaments and invite family to participate in decorating Nathaniel's tree. We decorate it on December 6 and leave it decorated until after Nathaniel's birthday on February 6. My daughter loves this tradition and is very excited each year to decorate Nathaniel's tree. She loves Christmas lights and loves that we have lights on until well after most lights are taken down. Each year, each participant picks out a new ornament for the tree. The ornament I pick each year reflects what I imagine Nathaniel would be interested in if he were with us. The first year was a shiny ornament, the second a race car, and so it will go on for years to come.

I did seek some grief groups for help and support. One group at the hospital focused solely on pregnancy losses. This group, though small in number, clearly understood the path that was before us. We shared tales of being at a store and trying to hold it together when the clerk asked why you would return such a cute baby shirt.

We went to another grief group that was more general. While this one was much more structured, some lessons were difficult to apply. When led to think through various memories of your loved one, we discovered the harsh reality that we don't have memories of our stillborn child.

> We discovered the harsh reality that we don't have memories of our stillborn child.

In general, this group was still beneficial for me. I found the leaders and participants eager to hear the perspective of child loss while maintaining compassion and empathy. The group helped each other through the stages of grief. As an introspective exercise, I appreciated the opportunity to process our journey through the stages of grief within a group.

A somewhat surprising help I discovered was being helpful

to others. In the midst of our all-encompassing grief, my wife and I were able to bless others around us. In the first year following Nathaniel's death, it seemed as though we heard of others who had experienced a loss way more than any other time. When we were three months into our journey of loss, finding a friend just beginning theirs and being the people that they could talk with was helpful to us. Other friends experiencing grief sought conversation as well. We were humbled that others wanted to talk to us about their similar struggles and journey. They and we were living through what no one would want to imagine. Even when we functioned at our worst, we held onto a supernatural joy of life that came from our faith.

A somewhat surprising help I discovered was being helpful to others.

We had received many things that weren't needed anymore, baby items that we could donate to be used immediately. Many of Nathaniel's clothes were exchanged for seasonally appropriate children's clothing to be donated to an orphanage. All the coupons that Toys"R"Us sends after one's due date were turned into gifts given to children in need and donated in Nathaniel's name. The coupons that started out as triggers for added grief now had a purpose and were welcomed.

We also decided to have a one-year-old birthday party for Nathaniel. We invited everyone who was instrumental in helping us in that first year. It was a way to say thanks to all our friends and to celebrate a little life that touched so many, even though he never took a breath. It was something to look forward to rather than dread. We asked anyone who wished to bring board books to donate to our local library.

As I look back and think of the pastor's comment about crowns,

I see crowns in many conversations. I see crowns in the donations made in Nathaniel's name. Crowns emerged as I went through a tough trial with my faith intact, coming through even stronger. And then, there are the bonding times I've had with family and friends.

Amazing how a little life touched so many people without needing to take a breath. The why me question, "Why must I face this world without my son with me?" has been replaced. Instead I now think, why not me? I have been given strength, shown compassion and seen blessings, all because of Nathaniel. It isn't easy, but with the hope I have, it is only part of the time that I wish it wouldn't have happened. I am who I am because of this experience. My faith says I will see Nathaniel again one day and spend an eternity with him in the presence of a good and gracious God. I will take the days here on earth missing Nathaniel while continuing to count the crowns until the day we are reunited.

*David Cooksey is husband to Amanda and father to two girls at home – Abigail, aged 6 and Felicity, aged nineteen months as well as dad to Nathaniel, born still at thirty-nine and a half weeks, just after his last scheduled prenatal check-up. David works in the medical device and healthcare industry, is active in church life and loves to be outside.*

# I RAGED AT GOD, AND THAT'S OKAY

### SARAH L. HAGGE

There is so much that I can't remember from the dark, early days of grieving the little girl I was not going to have a chance to raise, while learning how to be a mother to my other tiny little girl. Yet, there is one sentence that a friend wrote to me that I can't forget. I clung to it white knuckled, like clinging to the steering wheel during a blinding blizzard. "I raged at God the day your girls were born". This friend had done the very thing I wanted to do. She was saying the words I felt were too taboo to think, much less to say aloud. She was angry. For us. With us.

Many people told me they were praying for us. I wanted to scream back, *"What for? People were praying for Naomi, and look how much good that did!"* I quietly thanked them. In my faith tradition, there is supposed to be power in prayer. Prayers are supposed to bring comfort and strength. I knew the people who told me they were praying for us believed in the power of prayer. I knew they were doing the absolute best thing they knew to help us. Most importantly, they were acknowledging the death of our daughter, and for that, I could not thank them enough. But prayer did not bring me comfort. I have prayed countless times in my life: for big and small stuff, for people to be healed and for rain to stop. Many times, I praised God when my prayers were answered in the way I had hoped. As many times again, I offered clichéd acknowledgements that we did not understand the bigger plan, or we may not always get the answer we want. That was no longer good enough.

For two years, we had tried to get pregnant. Three times my heart had been broken for the babies we lost during early miscarriages. During thirty-six weeks of pregnancy, my body had given everything it could

> Prayers are supposed to bring comfort and strength... but prayer did not bring me comfort.

give to nurture twin girls: my two strong and courageous girls. And then, Naomi was taken from us. She was perfect. Beautiful. She had a head full of dark hair. There were no reasons and no answers. At best, prayer felt useless. At worst, it was a slap in the face: a cruel reminder of the daughter I was not permitted to raise.

I withstood the responses from others extolling the blessings from God that I had in my little survivor, Lydia. I would turn away thinking, I know better than most how precious her life is. Of course, she is an incredible blessing. She is the light of my life. The joy of her being here and my thankfulness for her being alive and well do not replace the unfathomable pain that the other greatest blessing in my life, Naomi, is not among us.

I knew I was supposed to find rest in the words people spoke and the images they shared. *Naomi is in a better place.* As her mama, away from me was not a better place. *She no longer feels pain.* I wanted to scoop her up and soothe her when she toppled over and hit her head. *Her great-grandma is rocking her.* I should have been the one rocking Naomi. *You will see her again, and you get to spend all of eternity with her.* I wanted to see her now, sitting up, rolling over, taking her first steps and saying her first words.

I heard people say over and again that everything happens for a reason, that it is all part of a plan we cannot understand. After living every day with grief that has cut me to my core, I cannot believe that. Things do not just work out. They do not always happen for a reason. And they certainly are not all for some greater good. I do not believe Naomi's death happened for a reason or greater good. The good that comes from it will be because we have worked to bring good from the pain: so that her short life will be remembered and celebrated.

> The death of my child forever altered my view of the world.

As I attempted to make sense of my faith in a world that no longer made sense to me, I felt like it was inappropriate for me to doubt, to question or to be angry. The death of my child forever altered my view of the world. My heart was irreparably broken. For bystanders, this was difficult to watch. Whether I wanted them to or not, others from my faith tradition stood on the sidelines, ready to rush in and help correct my course. I made up excuses for not attending services. I could not read anything, much less scripture. I could not pray. I was angry. I seethed as people around me praised God for answering their prayers for material things, while I sat twice a month with other parents whose pleadings with their God to save their child went unanswered. Yet, it seemed that all of the other bereaved parents around me found strength in their faith, while I only found flaws. Where had I gone wrong?

Over the course of the past year, I have worked to be gentle with myself. I have fought against the guilt of not feeling the things I am supposed to feel or doing the things I am supposed to do. Gradually and haltingly, I am learning to let go of believing what others tell me is right and embracing the desire to find what I believe is true. My anger is dissipating while more complex and nuanced emotions fill its place.

Some people find comfort in and overcome the sting of death by turning towards their faith. Others question, doubt or turn from their faith as part of the work of grieving and healing. We all grieve in different ways; there is no right or wrong. So today, if you are in the latter camp, I want to tell you that is okay. Come sit with me, and shed the pretence that all is well. Rage. Question. Doubt. Seek. Run. Find. I will not pretend to have the answers. There is no deadline on your grief and no end point for your questioning. Take the time you need to find what is true for you. You were forced on a journey you never wanted to travel. Whatever place of faith or lack thereof you arrive at, it will be borne out of courage and strength. It will be forged by the deep love for your child and honed through the process of healing. I can think of nothing more authentic.

*Sarah L. Hagge and her husband are parents to twin girls, Naomi – unexpectedly born still – and Lydia. The friendships formed with other bereaved parents have helped Sarah survive, and she hopes to be able to do the same for others.*

## SECTION SIX

# STILL MOTHER

## STILL THEIR PARENT; STILL MY CHILD

# THE INVISIBLE MOTHER

## SOPHIE MCAULAY

A tiny boy came into this world in silence, on a misty December morning not long before Christmas. Born at twenty-two weeks' gestation, he was extremely premature and just too small. He did not survive birth.

My waters had broken about a week before, for unknown reasons, and I spent several days in the hospital as doctors scrambled to convince my husband and me that our baby was not going to survive, and we should abort him. Despite the fact that our boy was still alive and healthy in my belly, the medical staff seemed unable, or unwilling, to give us any hope.

One doctor said to me, "The next pregnancy will have a better outcome".

The next pregnancy? I was still pregnant and could not take in those cruel and confusing words. How could I possibly relate to a future pregnancy when I was still pregnant? How could we possibly know that a subsequent pregnancy would turn out better, or if there would even be another pregnancy?

Noel was conceived with the help of IVF, after we had failed for years to get pregnant on our own. There was simply no way of being certain whether we would be successful again, nor what risks would be involved. I pleaded for help. I was not willing to give up on our child. Yet, no one wanted to listen.

Before we left the hospital without our son, a doctor tossed a brochure about miscarriage to me. It mostly talked about early miscarriage, when you have cramping and bleed out the remainder of the pregnancy. But I gave birth to a *child*. A child. What did that piece of paper have to do with me? I had looked at my son's beautiful face, touched his soft skin and seen that he looked like me. We named him Noel. He had ten fingers, ten toes, dark hair on his head and looked perfect. Noel was our son, our flesh and blood! That piece of paper was of no help to me. Worse, it conveyed to me that the doctor did not consider our son a real child, rather just a pregnancy that could easily be replaced.

> How could I possibly relate to a future pregnancy when I was still pregnant?

Coming to grips with how to mother my stillborn son has been an incredible challenge. He was my first – and perhaps only – child. Before he was born, I knew nothing about being a mother. There was no one to teach me how to go about being a parent to a child who rests in a grave instead of in my arms. For the first few months, I even imagined that it would have been harder had he lived for some time. People told me that as well.

It soon became apparent that I was supposed to go back to being the person I was before being pregnant with him, as if my life had not changed. It was true that on the outside my life was much the same. Our IVF journey continued after a few months' break, with mood-altering hormone injections, painful egg extractions and the disappointment that inevitably follows the negative tests. I went back to swimming, my favourite form of exercise, and I took a trip to Italy with my husband. To those around us, it seemed as if we had both continued with life like it was before Noel. Nothing could be further from the truth.

I was lost. I had a son, but nobody could see him. I saw him, though: in my dreams and in my nightmares. I felt him kicking inside me several months after he was born silent. The crib, pram and clothes we had prepared for him, he never used. Our two cats at home never got to meet their human brother.

Infertility circles use the term *involuntarily childless*. Childless, without children. Yes, I suffer from infertility, yet I do have a child. As far as the fertility treatments went, however, we were still considered childless, which in turn warranted us doing more treatments. Of course, the goal was to become pregnant again as soon as possible. With each treatment, I felt an increasing sense of guilt. Guilt that I was trying to replace Noel, when I really just wanted him to have a sibling, and for me to have a living child to parent. Anxiety crippled me. People around us urged us to try again, as if that would immediately remove the horror of losing Noel and make life good again. Perhaps they were hopeful that a living child would make me forget that my son was dead? Perhaps I hoped for that, too.

We lost touch or fell out with the majority of friends and family. Cruel comments that insinuated that Noel's death was not something worth grieving came in a steady stream. Both spoken and unspoken expectations that I ought to be happy and grateful for what I had took a toll on me. People who used to be my friends turned away when they saw me in the street, or looked away when I answered honestly their questions about how I was doing. I was told not to cry, that I had to be strong, as if the two are mutually exclusive. Rather than continuing to fall short of people's expectations, I withdrew from them to conserve my precious and very limited energy. I only did the things I wanted to do and avoided what increased my anxiety and made me uneasy,

> I gave myself permission to feel, to stop pretending that I was fine with being forced to justify my feelings.

like family dinners and birthday celebrations. That included avoiding children any way I could for a long time. I gave myself permission to feel, to stop pretending that I was fine with being forced to justify my feelings.

I choose whom I tell about Noel and how much. It is kind of a double-edged sword because when people talk about their children, I want to tell them about my boy. How I see him at the age he would be now. How I picture what he would look like and be like. Instead, I rarely say anything. His milestones are missing from the narrative of my life as his mother. In addition, telling strangers about him means letting people know that he died. Although there is nothing wrong with doing that, I do think death is discomforting and scary to most people, especially if you yourself have not been touched by it. Noel's story is intimately connected with death. I crave to talk about and experience the ups and downs of motherhood, but I struggle with the feeling that mine are just the tragic details of someone else's life no one wants to hear about. Life without him is hard. There is no way to sugarcoat it.

Holidays have taken on a completely new meaning since I became a mother to my stillborn son. His birthday is the most important day of the year, as I imagine it would be had he lived. Even though it hurts like mad, and the day is filled with anguish and endless sadness, we celebrate it with balloons, cake and gifts at Noel's graveside. He gets his own little Christmas tree, Easter decorations, candles and pumpkins for Halloween, fresh flowers all throughout the year. I love doting over his special place; it is the one thing I can do for him now. It makes me feel like his mum.

I cannot remember exactly when things became a little lighter. It was not as if I woke one morning, and suddenly could hear the birds sing and was able to breathe again. Yet, it did happen. Slowly, some friends came into our life, new ones mostly. I found people who share a similar story, and leaned on them, shared Noel with them.

**His milestones are missing from the narrative of my life as his mother.**

I take care not to be around people who disrespect me or my son, as they have no place in my life. I take part in creative projects. They were difficult at first because they brought the grief to the surface once again, but they have also acted as a catalyst for healing. It has become another way for me to honour him and process my loss. On his gravestone, it says, "You are always with us", and he is always present in a spiritual way, even though he cannot be seen.

Our efforts to give our son a sibling have not yet been successful. I do not know how I will feel if I have to live the rest of my life without any living children. I suspect I will have to find a way to survive that as well. A sliver of hope that we will get pregnant again remains, but not everyone goes on to have other children after child loss. That never occurred to me that first year after Noel's birth. I think I just assumed it would happen, that not having more children was just the stuff of cruel nightmares. But then again, it never occurred to me that I would have to watch my husband, the love of my life, carry our son's tiny white coffin in his arms, on the way to the funeral. Nor did I think I would survive that day, but I did and continue to do so.

No, this is not the life I had imagined, and gratitude has been a difficult emotion to feel after the loss of so many dreams. Anger, bitterness and sadness seem to be the more natural emotions of the grieving life. The hurtful things people have said continue to hurt and confuse me, but they do not define me as a person; I do. Besides, I can only take responsibility for my own actions. I will continue to feel an incredible amount of gratitude that I had Noel and for the few memories we made with him; of him. The kind of gratitude I think you can only feel when you have experienced loss. He is my son. I am his mummy. No one can do a better job of loving him than I can, and that I will never feel embarrassed about.

*Sophie McAulay is a photographer with a background in archaeology, and a creative soul. She loves to travel with her husband Antony, and together they celebrate the life of their only child Noel James by bringing Noel's Spirit Teddy along on all their journeys. Sophie participates in annual grief-centered art projects as a way to heal and incorporate Noel in her life.*

# GRIEF IS A JUGGLING ACT

## SAMANTHA MEDAGLIA

With grief, there is no such thing as "getting over it". Bereaved parents simply learn to adapt to their new reality and how to face life going forward. Like any other grief, this is a journey that differs from person to person.

In February, we lost our daughter, Grace, when she was born still at twenty-four weeks' gestation. In the beginning, the shock of our sudden loss helped manage the inevitable pain since it all felt like a horrible dream. As my due date came and went, the reality that we would not get to know our daughter became despairingly real.

Our grief came in waves. It still does. Early on, we felt as though we were drowning in a sea of darkness, with no sign of shore in sight. There were days when we felt strong and proud to be her parents; then there were days that felt impossible. As reality set in and our loss became real, the healing also began. Today, we are experiencing smoother sailing as we find hope while we navigate our way through this new version of life.

My husband Genio and I reacted both similarly and differently at the same time. When we first came home from the hospital empty handed, I felt lost and as though my life had lost meaning. I no longer knew what the future had in store for me in the days, months or even years to come. As I struggled to find my purpose again, my initial reaction was to dive in and find ways to raise awareness and share my daughter's story. I very quickly owned the title of bereaved mother, and I vowed to always be Grace's voice and make her proud.

> We felt as if we were drowning in a sea of darkness, with no sign of shore in sight.

Genio's process was different. He became much more introverted and kept to himself, pulling away from friends and family, avoiding the subject almost entirely. To this day, he still chooses to experience his grief on his own, and he has found his own sources of comfort and distraction.

While I can't speak much about my husband's journey, I can say that my own has been enlightening. Since losing my daughter, I find myself driven to make her proud. I now realize I had taken many moments of my pregnancy for granted. Since losing Grace, I have done as much as I can to honour her and be someone she would be proud to call Mommy if she were here with us.

One thing Genio and I do together is set aside certain times and occasions to celebrate and remember her. This is something my husband and I will always have in common. Even though our journeys have been so different, I know that we can always honour Gracey together.

It took some time for me to make sense of what we were going through. The first week of being home from the hospital, I stumbled across a Facebook group for anyone who has experienced loss of any kind. The group, Ink and Paper Healing, included a month-long challenge in which we were given different prompts each day. The prompts were designed to help us to express and face our grief and begin the healing process. For some, this meant thirty days of drawing; for me it was thirty days of letters.

> It has been said that children change everything, and I now know that this is no less true when they are gone.

I looked forward to the time that I gave myself to write each day and the prompts we would receive. I know that setting aside time to write each day helped me establish a routine that allowed me to honour and acknowledge our Gracey every day. Since the completion of that month, I have continued to keep a journal in which I write to her each day. It has been a source of comfort, documentation of my love for her and acknowledgement of my feelings as I grieve. More recently, I have been able to return to my letters and use them to write and speak publicly about my loss.

I have become increasingly aware that pregnancy and infant loss are not often recognised as a significant loss by anyone other than those who have been touched by it in some way. The sad truth is that in society, this type of loss is still a taboo subject, and that has led to a world full of uninformed citizens. A large part of what has helped me work through the difficult times has been advocating on behalf of women who have experienced this type of loss and raising awareness about pregnancy and infant loss.

The ability to channel pent-up energy into something productive and positive has helped me avoid falling into a deep darkness. The hardest part is accepting that at this point in my journey, people expect me to feel or *be* a certain way. As a friend recently pointed out, we can't control our feelings, but we can choose what we do with them.

On the harder days (they come less frequently now), I allow myself time to be sad and embrace the hurt. I have learned to expect those days at certain times: her birthday, Christmas, my due date. I acknowledge that the sadness I feel is warranted, that I shouldn't be ashamed and that it only proves my love for my daughter. Instead of fighting, I embrace the sadness and allow myself time for self-care. Sometimes this means a day at the spa; other times it may mean a day of extra writing. Whatever my heart and mind tell me I need at that moment, I listen.

On the other hand, when I am having a good day, I embrace it as well. At times, I feel guilty for allowing myself to be happy. Then I remember that I would have raised a daughter who would want me to choose happiness, and I dedicate my smiles to her. I focus on the positive and welcome opportunities to acknowledge Gracey and show my love and pride for her in uplifting ways.

Grief is a juggling act. It is the process of finding balance among acknowledging, feeling and accepting our loss, while learning how to incorporate those feelings into our new life. Helping others has been a huge part of my healing process. I completed a grief facilitation course in order to support others through losses of their own while honouring and being able to speak openly about my personal experiences. I choose not to hide my daughter's story, but I find comfort and peace in sharing her with those around me. I know that the ability to do so has helped me get to where I am today.

I was meant to raise a daughter and watch her grow, but losing her has made me grow in ways that I never knew possible. It has been said that children change everything, and I now know that this is no less true when they are gone.

*Samantha Medaglia graduated from Professional Writing at Algonquin College in Ottawa, Canada. Since losing her daughter Grace to stillbirth, she has been driven to help others on their grief journeys and has recently been certified as a grief facilitator. She hopes to support others while honouring her own loss.*

# SURVIVING THE LOSS OF MY LONGED-FOR FIRST CHILD

## REBECCA HARRIS

I am writing this exactly eleven months after losing my precious son, James. He was born at full term and was utterly perfect, but the onset of labour prompted a blood vessel in his placental membranes to rupture (a condition known as vasa praevia) causing him to lose around half his blood. He was delivered in shock by emergency caesarean section, revived and received blood transfusions over the course of the next few hours. But he was not able to recover. James died in my husband's arms at the age of nineteen hours.

The loss of our baby was an enormous shock. Nearly a year later, the shock continues in many ways. We were as prepared as we could be for the birthing and bringing our little one home. We never imagined we would be preparing his funeral just a few days later.

James was our first baby. We had struggled with infertility for approximately two and a half years before becoming pregnant in our first round of IVF. I had reached the point where I didn't think I would ever see a positive pregnancy test. As the pregnancy progressed and we received assurances that all was well, we began planning our new life together. Everything was falling into place. We had purchased a house just before I became pregnant and began to plan our next chapter. Becoming a family would make our lives complete. When I look back, I remember my pregnancy as being full of immense joy and hope for the future. It was the happiest time of our lives.

The first month of our loss is a blur. Time played tricks on us. Nothing seemed real. We wrote down everything we could remember about my pregnancy and the incredible day we had with our beautiful son. We didn't want to forget anything about him. My husband didn't cry much in the first few weeks, but the grief manifested itself physically, and he suffered terrible back pain for the first time. I was incredibly sad that my baby had gone from me, and I pored over his photos and videos every day.

## We didn't want to forget anything about him.

The reality of our loss began to hit the second month. The sadness worsened, and I fell into despair. The agony of being apart was terrible, and I didn't want to live without him. I felt so low and desperate I didn't know how I would get through the grief, the overwhelming sense of loss or ever be able to feel any joy in life again. Not only had we lost our precious baby and all that he would have brought to our lives, but we had lost our innocence, our identity as parents and the future we had desperately wanted. I no longer had a purpose in life. I questioned everything about life and death. I was certain I was going mad. I started writing a journal to help process my thoughts and make some sense of my feelings.

A few days after we lost James, we discovered that vasa praevia can be detected by ultrasound before birth, which meant that our son's death was preventable. Guilt gripped me; I should have done more for him. I was on the verge of a nervous breakdown, so we decided to reach out for help. We contacted a bereavement charity that offered individual counselling. Making this initial step gave us much needed relief.

The counselling helped us immensely. We could unburden our feelings to someone besides each other. We were lucky to feel at ease with our counsellors immediately. They were interested in hearing about our son, which was enormously comforting.

> I have come a long way from the intense grief I felt in the first few months.

My counsellor told me there is no right or wrong in grief, it has no timeframe and no instruction manual. My infertility was a big issue for me. I was worried we would never have a family, but my counsellor helped me realise that my fear was irrational, and I had every reason to be optimistic. She encouraged me to hang on to every last shred of hope and not let it go. She gave me thoughts to consider and tools to help me, such as when and how to tell James's story.

Since we lost James we haven't socialised much, but we have spent more time with friends who don't have children to maintain a social life we feel comfortable with right now. It can be painful to be reminded of the life we should be living. In time, we hope to rekindle all our friendships again. I made contact on social media with other parents who could identify with our situation and knew our pain. It helped to know we were not alone. We attended a support group, but it wasn't helpful because we weren't able to process anyone's grief besides our own. I found it helped to take it one day, or even one moment, at a time and not expect too much of myself or anyone else. We needed to do what was right for us.

I have come a long way from the intense grief I felt in the first few months. The grief has eased a bit; I can manage it to a degree. I think the process would have taken longer had I not had the support of a counsellor. I still struggle, but I have learned ways to cope. Exercise and walks in the country are a great way to clear my head and generate a different perspective. The countryside is peaceful, and nature offers a temporary escape. Simple things like watching the birds, observing the changing seasons and watching buds growing on the trees have been healing and have helped me see some beauty in life once again.

My husband's and my walks led us to seek a challenge in memory of James. We embarked on a nine-day hike for charity the day James would have turned six months old. We raised more money than we anticipated, and friends and family joined us along parts of the route. This proved to us how much our little family mattered to others and gave us a sense that we are not alone in our grief. It also gave us a great sense of achievement for our little boy. We are determined to help others by continuing to raise awareness of vasa praevia, and I am involved with a charity focused on campaigning for screening for the condition.

**Another coping mechanism has been finding ways to remember James.**

Another coping mechanism has been finding ways to remember James. The thought that he would be forgotten made me very anxious in the months after he died. I felt I was betraying James when I wasn't thinking of him, and it became exhausting. Physical reminders helped with this: we have his photos and objects that remind us of him all around the house. I wear his fingerprint on a necklace. I don't rely on the physical reminders to remember him, but I find comfort knowing they are there, and I smile when I see them.

James is never far from my mind. He lives in my heart, and I know he will never leave me. James is also in all the plans I am seeing through, which were made when I was pregnant with him, especially plans for our new house. He is in all the plants I planted and nurtured when he was alive in my belly, and in those gifted to us after he died. I have watched them grow this year, and I will do so for many years to come. He is a part of nature; he is the colour of the sunset and the twinkle of the stars. I associate several things with James; the colour lilac, so when given a choice of colours I pick lilac or purple; sunshine, so I think of him when the sun warms my skin; and birds of prey, particularly buzzards, as one was circling overhead when we took James into our garden on the day of his funeral. They make me smile and think of him.

It is important to celebrate our son's life, to acknowledge he was here and that he is loved and always will be. We have found rituals to be helpful. Every night, we wish James a good night and tell him we love him. We visit his grave in our village almost every day. It is where we feel closest to James, and talking to him there gives us comfort. When we visit new places, we buy a trinket for him. It makes us feel that he is included in our lives. Our first trinket was a heart shaped stone. We repeat a ritual of leaving it with him for a few days and then taking it to put on my bedside table for the next few and so on. We sometimes put it in our pocket, and we tell James where it has been. It helps to continue our bond with him and brings us comfort.

Early on after James' death I was desperate to know if I could survive this devastating loss; it is now several months down the line and I am surviving. I still feel incredible sadness about James. Some days I still yearn for him. On those days, the rituals and reminders aren't enough; yet I believe I have come a long way from where I was. The love of family and friends, and finding what comforts me brings the light slowly back into my life, which I didn't think would ever happen again. We still have to navigate our first Christmas without James, which will trigger so many memories of last year as we waited for his arrival. This is then followed shortly by his first birthday. I know I want it to be a day of celebration for his life, and I hope to make the cake I would have lovingly made if he were here with us.

In time, I hope the happiness James gave me will become much more poignant than the sadness. He has made me look at life through different eyes and makes me appreciate things I used to take for granted. He has taught me what it feels like to be a parent. He will always be my son, and I will always be his mother. Nothing can ever take this away, not even death. I am slowly finding that there is more to live for. If I am brave and I look, I will find "the more". I know James would want this for both of us.

*Rebecca Harris lives with her husband in the countryside in Herefordshire, UK where she enjoys immersing herself in nature. Rebecca is passionate about spreading awareness of vasa praevia and campaigning for screening after losing her healthy full-term son, James, soon after birth. She hopes her writing will inspire and bring comfort to others navigating the journey of child loss.*

their
existence
is as real
as their
absence

# GROWING YOUR FAMILY

## PREGNANCY FOLLOWING LOSS

# TRYING AGAIN DOES NOT MEAN I FAILED

## AMANDA RUSSELL

"Try again soon, okay?"

These were the words spoken to me by my mom as she hugged me on her way out the door.

My sister repeated the sentiment. "You really should try again".

Twenty-four hours earlier, we had laid my son to rest. One week after his birth. His very silent birth.

The me right now, the me who is writing this, would probably be outraged if someone told anyone to "try again" after only one week of losing their baby: the day after that baby's funeral. In my experience, people were obsessed with the idea of our trying again for another baby. A new baby. I know that saying those words so soon after loss can feel like an attempt at replacing the baby who died. Those words can minimise the child that was. I know the good intentions behind those words despite the sting of them. I know that people offer advice and platitudes as a way to show their love and as a way of helping.

It has been important for me to hold on to this knowledge throughout this past year. It's what allowed me to smile at my mom and at my sister and simply say, "We will". I understand now that they only wanted what's best for me. But I couldn't see that then.

When Ryan died, a piece of me floated away, and I wasn't quite sure how to function as a whole person. That incapability protected me from dangerous comments like theirs. The comments were meant to help and heal. In hindsight, they were only band-aids to the greater problem that couldn't be fixed with words.

Those words, "try again", made their way into my mind and became the central focus on my journey through that first year.

One night, a few weeks later, I sat hunched over my dinner plate. I pushed a few peas back and forth, and again heard the words in my head: "Try again".

With tears in my eyes, I looked at my husband, "You want to try again, right?" Until then I hadn't even considered that we wouldn't have another baby: that maybe my husband would be too scared to make the attempt. With tears in his eyes, he replied, "Of course I do. I just didn't want to push you".

With this bit of encouragement from my husband, I felt a sense of purpose for the first time in weeks. I resolved to speak with my doctor at my six-week appointment about this "trying again" business.

When that day came, the doctor and I talked about my physical and emotional healing. We talked about what happened to Ryan.

And then I asked, "Can we try again?"

She replied, "Physically, you are capable of trying again. There is no reason you shouldn't be able to have another healthy pregnancy".

Then I saw the flicker of worry in her eyes. "But you should wait until you have properly grieved. You need to grieve fully, so your next pregnancy won't be too stressful".

Now I had conflicting advice. Those who said to "try again" and those who said to "wait". My doctor left me with a lot to think about. Two things she said in particular stood out to me. The first was how I should properly grieve before getting pregnant again. A perfectionist by nature, I badly wanted to make sure I was grieving the right way. I wasn't in therapy or group support. Neither had appealed or worked for me, so I had been working through my grief with my husband and a few women I had met online and through friends. Was this the proper way? I had no idea. But it was my way, and it had been helping so far. That seemed enough at the time.

The second was that I should grieve fully. This was problematic for me. If something is full, it will have a stopping point. An ending. How was I supposed to know when my grief had ended? As far as I could tell, six weeks into my grief, I believed there would never be an end. I would love my son forever; therefore, I would grieve his loss forever. Over one year later, I still believe this to be true.

## How was I supposed to know when my grief had ended?

I fully grieve by keeping my son present in my life. My husband and I light candles, celebrate Ryan's milestones, fill our home with tokens of him and do other beautiful things to remember our son. I do these things as much today as I did one year ago. I am constantly grieving. So by this logic, was I never to try again if my grief would never be fully completed?

I grappled with these thoughts all the way home and for the rest of the day as I waited for my husband to get home from work. I had conflicting advice, but what it came down to was my needing to trust myself: to know my heart and what my heart needed.

When he walked in the door, I told him the news.

We were going to start "trying again".

I wish there was another word for it. When you "try again", there's an implication that you failed the first time. I want to be clear for myself and for every other woman out there who has ever been able to "try again" after losing a baby during pregnancy or after: We did not fail. We loved, cared for and cherished our babies more than anything on earth. That is not failure. That is all a mother can do. And we did it.

Eventually I stopped saying "trying again" and replaced it with "trying to grow our family". There was no hint at loss or failure in that phrase, and that became so important to me.

Ryan isn't defined by just his loss. He isn't this failure in my life. He's a part of the family and any baby coming after him would be an extension of our family. A family that Ryan began.

So there we were. Barely two months between us and the death of our firstborn. Trying again.

It was hard. Emotional. Scary. And it was work. We both wanted it even more than I think either of us realised at the time. We put a lot of pressure on it. We were married for nearly four years before we had Ryan. We were so ready to grow our family. When that positive test came, four cycles later, the emotions I was hit with were so intense. Relief mixed with fear. Joy mixed with anxiety. And, oh boy, there was guilt.

For me, trying again, and then being pregnant again, during the first year of grief came with a lot of guilt. Guilt that I wasn't devoting myself enough to my son who died. Guilt that on the outside it would appear as if I had moved on. Guilt that I was maybe somehow being irresponsible because we had lost Ryan, and I knew now that there were no guarantees with pregnancy.

And when my second son was born, living and breathing, just after Ryan's first birthday, the challenging emotions didn't go away. There is so much joy in having this little boy here with us, but there will always be a little bit of hurt, too.

The thing is, my grief journey that first year took me on a lot of challenging paths. The paths set me up to face every new challenge that comes my way. I made a lot of tough choices. And I didn't always do things the way others wanted me to. Maybe I didn't do things the way my mom or even my boss at work would have liked. I know I didn't do things in my doctor's timeline. I did things in my own time. I worked with my husband to create a path that worked for us. And sometimes, even though we are partners in this journey, I had to walk that path in a different way than him. But that's what made it right for me. For us.

Trying again when we did… Getting pregnant again when we did… Seeking advice and then choosing whether or not I took it… I have made my grief journey my own. I do what is right for me. That's all any of us can do. We trust ourselves. My heart took me on this beautiful and emotional journey of "trying again". This baby I have here in my arms doesn't diminish Ryan's existence. Instead, I look at him and see pieces of my Ryan and I feel some peace. Finding the courage to try again during the first year brought me here, to this peaceful place.

No, trying again does not mean I failed the first time. Trying again reveals my courage. It gives life to my determination to give Ryan a sibling here on earth. Trying again allows me to take control of my grief. I will always be proud and grateful that I did.

*Amanda Russell is an English teacher who has found great comfort in words since the death of her firstborn son. She lives in Ontario, Canada, with her husband, her dog and her two boys: one in her arms and one in her heart.*

# THE BIG BROTHER HE WILL NEVER KNOW

## CHIARA GIOMMARELLI

More than a year has gone by since the death of our baby boy, Ethan. My husband and I sit on our sofa holding our second son, Aidan, who is fast asleep. As we hold Aidan, I recall holding Ethan's tiny, lifeless body. I remember sitting on the hospital bed and thinking how much I wanted to be a mum and experience all I had read and heard about. Was it just a bad dream?

Ethan was cute. Even now, I remember how nice his little head and hands were. It wasn't possible that such a beautiful being had no life. It was hard to hold him knowing he would never look at me again. Ethan would never wiggle in my arms. I would never hear him cry... that curious fact affected me more than anything.

Parents say that the moment they hear that first cry, they are hooked. Then they realise the baby somehow grabbed hold of Mum or Dad's little finger because the baby is scared and wants to be reassured.

We didn't hear our baby boy cry, but we held him while he passed away, and he held onto our fingers. We were scared as well. He was holding our fingers as if to say, "It's okay, Mum; it's okay, Dad. I will be all right and one day we will meet again".

We held his tiny hands and told him how much we loved him; how much we wanted him to stay. We prayed for a miracle that, all of a sudden, Ethan would survive. But it wasn't meant to be for us, so we held and kissed him goodbye. In that final kiss, I tried to let him know how much he was loved and how much he was going to be missed.

When I look at Ethan's brother, I sometimes wonder how it would have been to rock Ethan to sleep, to have fed Ethan.

How did we decide to try again for a child after such a heartbreaking event? I remember lying on the hospital bed looking at my then-fiancée, Richard, and thinking how much I loved him. I knew in that simple moment that I wanted to try again. I told Richard I wanted to have a baby and be able to take that baby home with us and watch that baby grow up.

**When I lost my child, I lost my innocence.**

I didn't give up on this dream, and the dream didn't give up on us. We waited a few months because I wanted to make sure I really wanted to be a mum and have a baby, that I was not just trying to replace Ethan.

Richard and I spent a lot of time together going to restaurants and on a few holidays. We started trying when we were in New York. When it finally happened, I was quite surprised. With Ethan, it took us nearly two years to conceive. This time it was just a few months.

I was home alone when I took the test. I stared at the Big Fat Positive sign. A large lump took hold in my throat. I felt light headed. So many thoughts rushed through my mind, but the loudest one was, "Can I really go through nine months of waiting, knowing I could lose this one as well?"

When I lost my child, I lost my innocence. I was no longer immune to what I read and heard. I was no longer naive. I tried my best to stay positive and look on the "bright side", but it was hard work.

The first time around, with Ethan, my thoughts focused on how to decorate his room, how many clothes the baby was supposed to have, which schools the child would eventually attend. I was obsessed with having the room ready, the clothes washed and all lined up in the drawers. I devoured books on how to bring up a child the Montessori way, how to make sure we would be the perfect family.

This time, I had none of that. The only thing I thought of was, "Please, God, do not take this one from me". I stopped working because my doctor was afraid the stress would have some consequences on my pregnancy. When I was halfway through the second trimester, I was no longer allowed to work.

When Richard and I first met with the doctor after the Big Fat Positive, the doctor told us I would eventually have to quit my job and stay home.

The doctor's words caused me to ask myself a lot of unhealthy questions. Did we lose Ethan because I worked too much? Did we lose Ethan because I didn't rest enough? What did I do wrong to trigger the loss of our first child?

I asked the doctor what I was and wasn't supposed to do, what I should and shouldn't eat. Friends, family, colleagues told me the doctor was right: I should be resting. That caused me to question my first pregnancy even more. Did everyone think that I worked and travelled too much during the pregnancy with Ethan? That I might have brought the loss on myself?

I asked the doctors if there was something I could have done to prevent losing Ethan: each doctor reminded me it had been unpredictable. There was absolutely nothing I could have done. Then I wondered silently, "Why do I have to stop working and rest, relax and take it easy if there was nothing I could have done?" The worry and relentless self-questioning stayed with me until the day I held our second son, Aidan.

What could I do this time that I didn't do before to secure a better outcome? I spent hours and days thinking about this. Finally, I reached the point where I told myself, "Enjoy this time off with the belly, because you do not know what might happen tomorrow". And so, I did.

It took me a few weeks to adjust, but in the end, I decided I was going to enjoy this new pregnancy and spend time with friends doing all the things I couldn't do while working.

It wasn't always easy to enjoy the pregnancy. When I later read some of my journal entries from the early days, I recognised my struggle. How do you honour the memory of a lost child while thinking about the new life growing inside you?

I had a meltdown while writing a pregnancy diary, because I was writing about my fears and compared those fears to the previous time. The breakdown came not because of the scary feelings, but because one day I would give the diary to our second child, and all I could think of and write about was the first one who died.

I felt so torn between the two worlds. How do I focus on the life growing inside me when all I can think of is the other baby I can no longer hold? The answer for me was to take it a day at a time. Some days I thought about the new baby; other days, despite my best efforts, I thought only about the child I had lost. And, yes, one day I will give Aidan the diary I wrote. He will have the opportunity to read about his brother, how I miss that brother every day. Aidan will discover that I was scared while carrying him, my second child.

Aidan will know about Ethan, the brother he never met, the brother he never fought with or played with. Aidan will learn much of my struggles through my writing. It was a very difficult pregnancy. I had a lot of internal turmoil, and the only actual resolution was to trust and believe this time around was going to be different.

Some people urged me to change doctors and hospitals, but I knew that Ethan's death had been no one's fault. There was no reason I should change the team. The day after Ethan died, our doctor had come into my room to talk to us. He sat with us and explained in detail what had happened. He was very emotional; Richard and I knew he really cared.

Some tend to believe that, for doctors, patients are just a number, another person on their schedule. But these doctors see us every month or more for the entire duration of the pregnancy. They somehow also bond with the baby. I remember looking at our doctor and knowing I could trust him. I knew that next time, he would be there no matter what. When we finally went to his office and told him I was pregnant, we discovered he already had a plan laid out for us that involved many doctors and visits to the hospital to ensure complete care.

It was not easy to walk those corridors in the beginning, because the only thought I had was, "This is where we lost Ethan". I saw familiar faces who had been there during the monitoring and dash for the operating room. My throat tightened. Could I trust them again? Could I have them deliver this child as well? The answer deep down was, *Yes I can*. Because it was not their fault; it was no one's fault.

Still I couldn't help holding on to some fear and worry, because no matter what we are told, we know things can go *wrong*. I experienced that wrong first hand.

But now, holding our rainbow baby, I know that things can also go well.

*Chiara Giommarelli was born in Milan, Italy, and moved to Belgium where she eventually found Richard, the love of her life, and Tyler their dog. They lost their son, Ethan, after complications during pregnancy. They now have a second child, Aidan, who will grow up knowing all about his big brother in heaven.*

# LABOURS OF LOVE

## CREATING MEANING AFTER LOSS

# TURNING GRIEF INTO LOVE

## KAREN PRISCO

Anger churned within me those first months after our baby's death. I vowed that I would exact vengeance on everyone I felt had failed me: the sonographer, the nurse who was supposed to help me birth and the priest from our church. I would find a way to make them pay for how I was treated. I vowed to never forgive the hurt I experienced. Most of all, I determined I would not be silent nor let them steal the good memories of my baby, even though her life was short.

Beyond the initial shock and grief of finding out our daughter, Elizabetta, had died around sixteen-weeks' gestation, I accumulated layer upon layer of hurt and anger. During my routine sixteen-week check-up, my midwife had difficulty finding a heartbeat. I was sent to the radiology clinic where the sonographer told me she couldn't find a heartbeat. I was informed I could leave and was given no further information or time to process what I had been told.

The following day, I saw a gynaecologist at the hospital who explained it would be in my best interest to terminate my pregnancy. I was given a date for a chemical induction. A week later I birthed our daughter alone in a hospital bathroom, because the nurse wouldn't listen to my history of rapid deliveries and wasn't available to be with me. I became very unwell due to the nurse's disregard for my concerns about the amount of blood I was losing, and I was unable to be present for most of the time I had with Elizabetta following her birth.

I had to be admitted overnight to stabilise my blood pressure instead of being discharged soon after delivery. As a result, I had to endure being asked by a nurse if I wanted Elizabetta placed in a refrigerator. To add to the hurt, our parish priest did not care for my soul or honour Elizabetta's life by visiting or helping organise a funeral. I still do not understand why he never offered any support or acknowledged our loss. I felt so

Beyond the shock and grief, I accumulated layer upon layer of hurt and anger.

angry, so hurt and so abandoned by my church. I contacted another church who welcomed me in my grief, and honoured Elizabetta's brief life and provided us with a sacred goodbye.

Because of well-intentioned comments people made that tore pieces off my heart and punched me in the stomach, I believed the world was against me. I felt very alone. I stifled everything into a knot inside me, bit my lip, said nothing and plotted my revenge. I needed to make someone accountable. I needed someone to hurt as much as I was hurting, and I knew screaming with rage in someone's face wasn't going to inflict the kind of pain I was feeling.

In the days and weeks after Elizabetta's death, I talked to other women and discovered my experience of birthing in the gynaecology ward was not unique. My heart broke, and I cried for each of them. I felt angry for them, and at them, while wanting to protect them and myself from the added suffering the hospital system had caused us. I felt as if these women had betrayed me by staying silent and not registering a complaint about the care they received after losing their child. I also understood they had been terribly hurt and in that hurt had found it too difficult to complain.

## I wanted her to be remembered with love, not wrapped in anger.

It didn't stop me from feeling that, in an indirect way, they had caused a portion of my pain and suffering.

I was exhausted. Anger and rage are exhausting. My maternal instincts had been awakened by that anger, and I needed to act. I carefully penned letters of complaint and sent them to the hospital and radiology clinic. I outlined the treatment I had received and recommendations for change; my need for vengeance had softened into a need to educate and reform. I knew in my heart of hearts that I could not carry my child, my sweet Elizabetta, if my heart was full of anger. I knew I wanted her to be remembered with love, not wrapped in hatred and anger. I also knew that trying to change the hospital through a complaint was next to impossible without a huge amount of energy and money, so instead of pursuing the complaints further, I decided I would try to change my approach.

I embarked on trying to heal my heart with kindness; I wanted to remember Elizabetta without the hurt and anger I carried. I wanted to heal the world and fix a broken hospital system that does not treat second trimester miscarriages as birthing a child. Most of all, I wanted peace.

From the day I discovered Elizabetta had died, I began writing. Because of the circumstances around her birth, I felt as if I had no one safe to talk to. The computer I gave the words to in the middle of the night when sleep eluded me did not offend me or judge my thoughts. The tears I shed were not seen as a sign of weakness, and they were hidden from my children whom I needed to protect from the full force of my grief.

The words flowed from my fingertips and flooded the computer screen. I realised I needed to add my voice to the conversation around baby loss. One of my poems starts:

> I used my voice and my hands to strip back the anger and hurt I felt.

"In the silence of your heart, I felt mine beat. In the silence of your cries, I found my voice". I had awakened to find a strength I needed to harness.

I used my voice and my hands to strip back the anger and hurt I felt. I slid into the world of baby loss and dedicated each spare moment to giving to other loss mums. I knitted and crocheted blankets for stillborn babies, sewed burial gowns and tiny nappies and shared my poetry on a Facebook page. I wrote to parenting publications asking them to publish articles on baby loss to help break the silence. I talked to anyone who wanted to listen, and most importantly, I listened to the stories of elderly women who had never spoken about their miscarriages or stillbirths. My heart nearly burst with the pain these women had carried for so long; yet, I still felt empty and alone. I needed to do more. I thought I could help heal myself by giving, but sometimes I felt resentful that few had given anything of themselves for me.

At the same time, I turned to a parenting forum to which I belonged. Someone sent me an article about a woman who had fundraised for a CuddleCot™. I felt this was something that I could focus on to enhance how women and their babies are treated in the hospital. The memory of Elizabetta being taken from me still hurts my soul. I wanted her with me, with her mama, cradled in my arms while I rocked her, so I could speak gently to her for as long as I could until I had to say goodbye. My heart raced as I realised that, if a cold cot were available, no mother would need to be asked, as I was, if she would like her baby placed in the refrigerator.

## Releasing the anger has allowed the tears I shed to be freeing instead of destructive.

My fundraising journey began. I started by asking for donations via Facebook and received donations from all over the world. I researched suppliers, shipping, customs and taxes, as the CuddleCot™ would be the first one available in New Zealand. An article was published in the local newspaper; more donations came in, and my fundraising target was met. Within six months of Elizabetta's birth, I had donated a cuddle cot to our local maternity hospital. Somehow, through the process, the anger I had surrounding Elizabetta's birth had dissolved. I felt as if I had made a positive change and had created a legacy for her. Other women contacted me about fundraising for their local hospitals. Slowly, a small ripple of love spread across the country.

I had somehow stumbled through a process of letting go of the anger and hurt I had built up and let consume me. I kept writing, which helped to order and process my thoughts and release them from my head when I tried to rest. Knowing that Elizabetta's name would be spoken and attached to gifts of love makes her memory sit a little gentler on my soul. Releasing the anger has made it easier for the grief to be felt in a positive loving way and the tears I shed to be freeing instead of destructive. My children have witnessed grief and love triumph over anger and hate. My teenagers softly tease, "Don't be mean to mummy, she will exact her vengeance upon you with love and kindness". They too have grieved, but they have witnessed and understand how powerful love can be. They have seen how much impact a small baby can have on the world and how each small act of love can heal one's heart and impact parts of the world which are broken.

*Karen Prisco is a full-time mum to her eight children. She lives in New Zealand and volunteers at a local Sands Group, as well as at the schools and clubs her children attend. An article she wrote on baby loss has been published in a parenting magazine, and she documents her journey through poetry.*

# WRITING MY WAY THROUGH GRIEF

## MEGAN WARREN

I am the mother of five boys, all of whom wanted to make their way into the world early. My eldest – now in his twenties – was born six weeks premature and spent his first three weeks in the NICU. Despite his early start in life, he is a happy, healthy young man who makes me proud. I am thankful to have him in my life. His brothers were not so fortunate; all my other pregnancies ended prematurely between twenty and twenty-three weeks' gestation. Three of our sons were stillborn, Brendan (twenty weeks), Kavyn (twenty-three weeks) and Alex (twenty-one weeks). Cianan was born at twenty-two weeks' gestation and lived for seven hours. The reason I went into premature labour – despite repeated testing – is unclear. Sometimes there are no answers.

When I think back to those early days of grief after the deaths of our sons, I remember feeling empty. I wasn't lonely. I had a good support network of family and friends, but none of them truly knew how I felt. The one constant after my experience of pregnancy loss was my journal. I had kept a diary all through my teens. In it, I shared all my teenage angst. Then one day my mother found my diary and read my innermost thoughts. I remember coming home from an afternoon with friends to find my bedroom door open and my diary lying on my bed. As soon as she knew I was home, my mother was standing at my door asking me questions that made it clear she had read my diary. I asked her if she had read it and she replied: "It was just lying there on the bed". I felt violated and betrayed. After that, I destroyed the diary and didn't put pen to paper for a long time.

> My journal was a release for all those feelings and emotions that could have stayed bottled up inside if I had not found an outlet.

Some years later while studying English at University, I was introduced to Tristine Rainer's *The New Diary* and the concept of journal writing. I learned that journaling differs greatly from the diaries I had kept in my teens. A journal could be anything I wanted it to be and could contain anything and everything that I wanted to include. I could record my creative writing adventures, notes about Christmas or my son, my goals and dreams or even my innermost thoughts. I could draw or sketch in my journal, stick in photos or mementoes of my day. Unlike my teenage diary, I could write as frequently or infrequently as I wanted. If I didn't have much to say, I would just record a short entry. This is how I began writing again.

It was only natural when our sons died that I would turn to my journal. I poured out my grief and frustration in that journal. It was the friend that I felt I didn't have. My journal was a release for all those feelings and emotions that could have stayed bottled up inside if I had not found an outlet.

As I prepared to write this essay, I revisited my journals. I found letters I had written to our sons. There were letters I had written to people who were less than supportive of our situation (letters that were never sent, but had released my anger and frustration). I found poems I had written about my experience. I found memories of my pregnancies and other meaningful interactions (some that I had forgotten). Those entries from the early days were full of anger, sadness and despair. There were pages with tear stains when I couldn't see a light at the end of the tunnel. As I read further into my journals, the entries became more hopeful and less dark and despairing.

Then there were the more positive entries that followed, where I wrote about my pregnancies. I told of changes I was experiencing as my body changed with the new life that I was carrying. I read again the hope we held for these pregnancies and our family's future. I wrote about each time we were faced with a challenge: test results that needed to be reviewed, preterm labour and hospitalisation to try to prevent preterm labour. I turned to my journal to record how I felt and the frustrations I had. I had little control over what was happening to my body, but my journal provided a means to express those frustrations. In one hospital admission, I journaled that I strongly requested the nurse put the cannula for the intravenous drip into my left hand. She did, but asked why it was so important. I told her: I am right handed. I want to be able to write and draw. Writing and drawing was one of the things that I could do while I was on complete bedrest.

> **I discovered that for me, the benefit gained from journaling far outweighs the negative aspects.**

You may be thinking, "I can't write". I'm here to tell you that YES, YOU CAN. You write shopping lists, emails and notes every day, even Facebook status updates. Writing in a journal is a variation of this everyday writing. To begin journaling, simply purchase a notebook and a pen. My personal preference is a notebook with a nice cover. When it comes to pens, I've used coloured pens, gel pens, ballpoint pens and – my favourite – fountain pens. Write about your pregnancy, about your baby, about what happened. Include quotes, scriptures, songs or poems that inspire you.

There has been much written about the therapeutic benefits of writing, including improvements in mood and psychological well-being, as well as general health. I have experienced the benefits of writing about my experience of pregnancy loss. Journals can be beneficial in helping others understand where we are in our healing journey. As a rule, I don't share my journals with anyone except for rare occasions with my husband or my counsellor. I do this when I have been experiencing a difficult time, and it was easier to let them read my journal entry than to verbalise those thoughts and feelings.

Journaling is not without intense emotions, especially when you write about traumatic experiences. Sometimes revisiting those traumatic events triggers upset and stress. I discovered that for me, the benefit gained from journaling far outweighs the negative aspects. Nothing will bring my sons back, but my journals can take me on a trip down memory lane, through the good times and through the bad times, too, and show me how far I have travelled on this road of grief and loss.

*Megan Warren is a wife and mother, living in Esperance, Western Australia. She is passionate about writing and creativity as an outlet for grief and loss. She facilitates mandala and creativity workshops in her local area.*

# SEW MUCH LOVE

## ARIANE AMANN

W hen I was younger, I thought we could just have our dream family whenever we wanted. I was so naive. Eight years down the road, I know better. Our first pregnancy ended in a silent miscarriage at twelve weeks' gestation. The second one with our first set of twins was not successful either – we decided to terminate it at twelve weeks due to anencephaly for both babies. After that and a lot of therapy for me, we got lucky. Our daughter Sarah was born healthy and full term, after a horrible pregnancy with gestational diabetes, cervical issues and a toxoplasmosis infection.

When I was ready to try for a sibling, we were hit with twins. Again. One did not survive past six weeks' gestation. Felix made it to twenty-three weeks when, due to cervical incompetence, labour set in. Felix died right after birth. You'd think I'd have been prepared for grief hitting me. I wasn't. At all. He was the only child that we lost and were actually able to hold, as the others were way too small to have anything left after the dilation and curettage those pregnancies had ended with. We now have a lively daughter, Sarah, and a little girl whom we're fostering.

The first year after Felix died was horrible. I did not think it would hit me that hard. I was already a member of the loss community, having mourned the loss of four babies before. I knew where to turn, what to do, what not to do. What I did not know was how deep "rock bottom" could be. For weeks after our little boy was born without a chance to live, my family, especially my daughter, was my only reason to get out of bed in the morning. I tried to give her a normal morning each day, including breakfast and play. After I took Sarah to kindergarten, I returned home, sat down on the couch and cried until I could cry no more.

**What I did not know was how deep "rock bottom" could be.**

When the pre-term labour had set in at twenty-three weeks' gestation, I learned that the hospital would take no measures to save Felix. He was too young, too small, too premature. He died right after they cut the umbilical cord, my husband Michael being with me all the time. At least we were both in the room when Felix came into the world and died. The thought of it all kept overwhelming me day by day.

In those first days, I made up my mind to sew some tiny clothes for Felix. I did not want him to be buried naked. I could not bear the thought of him lying in the ground without something to warm him. I needed a couple of days to decide what to do and in the end, I found myself in a fabric shop telling the owner in a shaky voice that I needed some fabric to sew for my dead baby. She helped me find the right things. I made a little shirt that tied in the front and tiny pants with feet. I also added a swaddling blanket to wrap around him. It took me about half a day to cut the fabric and sew it together. I could have been faster, but I took my time to take every step consciously.

I handed the things to our undertaker when she visited us a couple of days before the funeral. She promised to dress him. At that time, I felt unable to dress him myself. The thought of having to let him go again was making me cringe, and I was very glad that the funeral director volunteered to do this for us. I now regret that decision, but have made my peace with that missed opportunity.

I never saw Felix in the clothes I made, but I took a picture of a doll his size wearing them as I finished the clothes just in time for the funeral. The doll I put the clothes on for the picture was as big as Felix was, just over twelve inches. I had measured him in the hospital, so I knew the size. The day before the funeral, I had set my mind on seeing Felix once more. That was three and a half weeks after he was born and died. I fought my way through German bureaucracy from the graveyard, to the hospital, to the morgue where the pathologist finally talked me out of looking at him again due to the decomposition.

The clothes looked beautiful, and they made me feel a little calmer about putting my baby son in the cold ground in European mid-October. These clothes were the last thing I could do for him while there was so much I could not do. I could make him feel loved wherever he was by putting some handmade clothes on him.

For a long time, I thought about what to do with that early feeling of accomplishment. There was a spark in me that had been kindled by the sewing with so much love that had nowhere to go. I love sewing, and I thought about other parents having to go through the same pain that we did and still do. I was pretty sure I could not sew tiny clothes again, as that had been one of the hardest things I ever did.

Even though it seemed easy at the time, it surely was not the craft that made me feel so exhausted after finishing. It was the notion that I was sewing clothes for my dead son. Then one day, it just occurred to me: Why not make swaddling blankets and some keepsakes for the parents? I thought about that for a couple of days, then decided on key fobs. I had made some for family members, sewing leftover pieces from the fleece I had used to make a swaddling blanket for Felix.

When we met Felix after he died, the hospital staff had wrapped him in a worn towel and placed him in a Moses basket. That didn't bother me at the time. We were grateful to be able to say hello and goodbye to him. That was not something we were able to do with his four siblings who had died before him. The nurses had probably worked with what they had, trying to treat him as well as they could. But weeks after he was buried, I thought the wrapping could have been done with a little more care and dignity.

> I realise anew that I am not alone in this. I will get through this.

The spark had grown to a small fire in the meantime, burning low but steady. I had gone back to work by then, leaving little time to think about anything else. I sent e-mails to hospitals with maternity wards to see if they would be receptive to donations. The first one replied within a couple of hours, telling me what a wonderful idea this was. I called and asked how many they would need. The hospital only accepted pregnancies that did not anticipate complications, so only needed a small quantity. It felt strange to talk about those numbers as if they were for a business venture. Each of those numbers represented a dead baby, and here I was taking notes on how many babies needed to be lovingly wrapped for their parents to say hello and goodbye.

The second hospital also readily agreed to accept some of my sets. The third hospital required a bit more effort. I had to find the right person to agree to my idea. I managed to "sell" my idea to a NICU nurse who did some sewing herself for the babies. She made cuddly toys and loved the idea: parents, in being given key fobs, would have something from the hospital. The sad thing is, hospitals in my area are completely under-equipped for stillbirths and premature babies too small to live. In order to spread the word, and maybe encourage others to grieve in silence a little less, I agreed to write articles about my donations. A professional photograph of me handing the sets to the lead midwife accompanied the articles.

## The pain of missing Felix will never disappear, nor should it.

The first time I returned to a maternity ward to deliver the packages with the sets, I felt as if I were a character in a flashback horror movie. The thoughts of babies fighting for their lives and parents fearing and praying for their babies was almost too much for me. One delivery included the hospital our son was born in. I kept my composure as I entered the NICU where I delivered the sets. I even made it through the thank yous and back out without looking at the babies in the rooms beyond the doors: the rooms where I would have wanted our son to be, to be able to fight for his life. But he was not, and the only way I would ever be in the NICU was in delivering swaddling blankets for babies who would not live. Several times, I swallowed hard and choked back tears. Only when I reached home did that madness fade away, realising that I had done something meaningful that might help other parents.

I have been making these blankets for over a year now. I experience immense peace in the sewing. As the machine turns these pieces of fabric into the swaddling blankets and key fobs, I realise anew that I am not alone in this. I will get through this. I like to believe that my thoughts infuse each blanket and enshroud the parents who hold their child in one of my blankets or as they fumble the key fobs on their way home.

I have a place in my home where I keep some spare blankets. When I see them every now and then, they still remind me of my babies who were gone too soon and all the other little ones that never saw their parents' home. The pain has diminished, but will never totally disappear. Now, that pain is accompanied by a deep sense of love.

To say the sewing saved my life would be an exaggeration. However, it was significant in my recovery in the aftermath of Felix's death. I had something to do, something with a purpose. Despite all I was going through, I still could get meaningful things done – for

**I got through the worst stages of my own grief, in my own way.**

me and for others. Soon self-preservation kicked in, and life went on.

Make no mistake, loss is present for me every day: when our daughter points out a cloud that she thinks Felix is sitting on; when I see twins because I lost two twin pregnancies; or when I see our foster daughter learning and doing all the things I thought I would see Felix learn and do. The pain of missing Felix will never disappear, nor should it. I got through the worst stages of my own grief, in my own way. Cutting fabric, sewing, giving the blankets away.

Felix and my memories connected to him will stay with me forever. Maybe the giving means something for other parents who see that their baby son or daughter is treated with love and dignity, even if he or she is no longer alive. If my sewing project comforts just one mom or dad in grief, it's all worth it.

*Ariane Amann is a freelance journalist in Barleben, Germany. She is a mother of seven children and mom to two. She enjoys sewing for her daughters and spending time with friends who understand her grief. The occasional yoga class helps ground her when things get difficult.*

you've
changed
my life,
i will make
you proud
of what
remains

# ALWAYS REMEMBERED

## WE ARE NOT SEPARATED BY DEATH

# FOUR DAYS WERE TOO FEW TO MAKE A LIFETIME OF MEMORIES

## LINDSEY LYNCH

I was pregnant with our second child. We were excited to become a family of four. We counted down the weeks until his due date just days from Thanksgiving. We daydreamed of what our lives would be like with a toddler and newborn baby: the hourly wake up calls in the middle of the night, functioning on a few hours of sleep, making time for our toddler, changing dozens and dozens of diapers daily, dealing with a fussy baby and learning to balance between meeting the needs of both a newborn and a toddler. We were ready to take on this new adventure, this new life, this new stage.

It was an exciting time in our house. We were thrilled about our son becoming a big brother. We felt like we were on top of the world. Nothing could have brought us down off this mountain. Things were great and life was going in the direction that we wanted it to. We were ready to add to our family. Until, that is, life decided to make a very drastic change. In an instant, my world was split in two: the before and the after.

Bradley David Lynch was born at twenty-eight weeks' gestation via emergency caesarean section due to low amniotic fluid, minimal foetal movement and an erratic heart rate. He came into this world on Wednesday, September 2 at 5:46pm at two pounds, thirteen ounces and fourteen and a half inches long. One of Bradley's diagnoses was Rh disease, an incompatibility between my own blood and his. That condition started the domino-effect of his declining health and ultimate death. He was a very sick baby, even in utero (though we didn't know it at the time).

In an instant, my world was split in two: the before and the after.

Bradley had a hard life. Within a few hours of birth, he had to have an exchange transfusion. When he was four days old, the neonatologist came into my hospital room and told us they had discovered he had a perforated bowel. We had two options: surgery on the bowel or compassionate care. That specific surgery was risky, especially in light of how sick Bradley was. Compassionate care meant being with Bradley, holding him, having our older son meet his brother and spending time together as a family before allowing him to die. This was the hardest decision my husband and I have ever had to make.

In Bradley's final hours on this earth, he was held by his mother and father. His older brother was able to meet him, see him and touch him. We were together as a family, for the last time here on this earth. Bradley left this world on Sunday, September 6 at 12:05pm, surrounded by his mom, dad and big brother, Zachery.

My son lived for only four very short days. During his time in the NICU, I didn't realise our time together was limited. I didn't realise we would never get to take him home. Many "firsts" were taken from us on that Sunday afternoon. We would never get to celebrate his first Thanksgiving, his first Christmas or first birthday. We would never get to experience what it would be like to have two living children. What we had believed life would look like was turned completely upside down.

The moment Bradley took his last breath, I couldn't see far enough in the future to see how I could survive this. How could I continue living? Why would I want to continue to live when my son just took his last breath on this earth? I watched the air leave his body while I continued to breathe. How is that fair? How is that even possible? As a mother, I was supposed to protect my children. Instead, I was letting him die.

In the first couple of weeks following his death, I didn't want to do any of my daily routine: wake up; make coffee; eat breakfast, lunch or dinner or anything that I routinely did before Bradley. In my mind, if I went back to my "normal" routine, it would mean I was forgetting Bradley, as if I were turning my back on him.

## Why would I want to continue to live when my son just took his last breath?

Over the next few months, I gradually went back to my normal daily routines. I tried to at least. I hoped that going back to what I used to do before would speed up my grieving and healing process. I wanted so desperately to feel normal again. I wanted others to treat me the same as they had before, but that didn't happen at all. It was the exact opposite. I felt the most alone and isolated that I ever have in my life.

Soon it was Thanksgiving and Christmas. Those holidays quickly came and went. I gave myself space. If I didn't want to attend a social event, I declined the invitations. Whether the ones hosting these events realised the reason or not, I wasn't worried about how they felt. Yes, that sounds selfish, but I was grieving my child. In that setting, it was okay to be selfish. I didn't worry about what others thought. The holiday season will always be one of the most challenging times of the year.

There isn't any particular thing that helped me survive my first year. I wish there was. I wish I could give you a handbook on how to survive the first year after losing your child. It would include a week-by-week, and month-by-month guide on how you will feel and how far along

> ## In those early months, I couldn't see into the future where happiness and sadness could co-exist.

you should be in your grief journey. You could flip through to page twenty-five on month six and read step-by-step instructions on what you need to accomplish to make it to month seven. I wish so badly it was that easy.

I wish I could tell you that as more time passes, it gets easier. Depending on the day, that might be true, but when grieving the loss of your child, emotions ebb and flow.

Some days I felt okay and experienced joy. The next day, everything I saw, heard or said brought me to my knees. Feelings even changed hour to hour. I know I will experience triggers for the rest of my life. Even many months later, I am still brought to tears. I still cry. I still grieve. I still miss him immensely. I still yearn for him.

I search for Bradley daily. I see him when small white feathers randomly appear. I see him in a sunset and in a sunrise. I see him in the clouds, the moon and stars. I sense him in a warm breeze crossing my face. I experience him everywhere. I search for him so I can feel close to him. I will search for him the rest of my life, because this is the never-ending love between a mother and her child. It is a love so deep, I needed only four days with him for the love to last a lifetime and grow stronger with the passing of time. Because of Bradley, my heart has opened, my soul has grown richer and I will always appreciate the small stuff. I have learned that joy and grief can live side by side.

In those early months, I couldn't see into the future where happiness and sadness could co-exist. I couldn't see the light at the end of the tunnel. That tunnel was long and dark and scary, but that light is there. Don't give up. Don't ever give up.

Finding ways to remember and honour my child has helped me survive the first year. On holidays, it has become a tradition for our family to make a trip to the cemetery, bring flowers and take pictures. For the second holiday season, I created a project called Bradley's Memorial Tree. This tree is filled with ornaments adorned with names of children who aren't in their parents' arms anymore.

> I will search for him the rest of my life, because this is the never-ending love between a mother and her child.

Shifting the focus from Bradley to these beautiful and precious babies brought an unexpected calm within me, and an overflowing love filled my heart. I wanted to do something for other parents who don't have all their children with them on earth. I know how lonely and isolating child loss can be, especially during the holidays. One of the fears of parents who have had a child die is that others will forget their child. I wanted to make sure that doesn't happen. Their children's names will be spoken in my house; they will be honoured and remembered.

Writing also helped me survive the first year. I write about how I am feeling, how I am grieving and how I am surviving his death. I have found writing to be therapeutic while helping to keep Bradley's memory alive.

Surviving and living this life after loss is, for me, about finding ways to incorporate my child into our everyday lives: remembering him, honouring him and making sure Bradley is not forgotten.

We who have experienced the death of our child will walk alongside you. We will hold your hand. We will sit with you. We will do this without hesitation because we were and are you. We walked that lonely road. We sat in darkness. We survived that first year.

*Lindsey Lynch lives in Southern California, USA, with her husband and two children – Zachery in her arms and Bradley in her heart. She is an avid runner, stay-at-home mom and a blogger writing about running, food and her grief journey.*

# EFFICIENT GRIEVING

## RACHEL LIBBY

After my son died, I considered writing a book called *Efficient Grieving: For Those Who Want to Grieve Right the First Time.* I wanted to get this grief thing over with, but do it correctly so that it would not pop back up years down the line. I tried to read a lot of books right after Oliver died in an effort to become well-versed and educated on the subject of grief. In reality, I skimmed a lot of books on loss and read just one life-changing book in its entirety. The general gist of grief literature is that there is no wrong way to grieve and that everyone has their own way to process grief as it best serves them. But that felt like a lie.

Surely, there had to be a right way, and if not a right way, at least one way that was better than the rest. I assumed drowning my sorrows in alcohol or other mind numbing substances would not be an efficient (or perhaps legal) method to overcome my sadness. I likewise knew that pretending the event had never occurred would not be the best way to succeed at grieving. Eliminating those and other such ill-advised methods, I was still left with a myriad of techniques to try in order to get through that first year in the most efficient way.

I thought the worst thing would be to arrive five years post-loss and realise I had skipped a step and would have to do it all over again. That would label me as a failure in this test called grief. I was determined to face my feelings head-on and conquer this whole grieving thing the first time. I didn't want to have it following me around forever, popping up like some persistent rash I failed to treat properly the first go-round.

I spent that first year doing all the things I thought were the most efficient and effective way of grieving. I was in a therapist's office exactly one week after I delivered Oliver, my perfect but silent full-term baby. The therapist listened and helped in her gentle way, keeping me honest through the first six months of life without my son. She encouraged me to let my husband grieve his way (even though I was sure my way was the right way). My husband and I joined a local support group three months after Oliver died and met the best people I wish we had never had to meet. I found out there is nothing better than sitting in a room with people who truly get it. People who are walking this road and proving every day that a life after loss is not only possible but worth living. These are the only people in the world who know me solely because I am Oliver's mother, a fact that fills me with pride and purpose.

We had chosen owl bedding for Oliver's crib. When faced with the task of creating a programme for his memorial, the image of a mother and baby owl on the cover seemed an obvious choice. Little did we know that we would be permanently attaching the symbol of an owl to Oliver and his memory. Soon enough, our home filled with owls from friends in faraway states and countries. It feels frivolous to note the necklaces and vases, the cards and pillows, the cookie jars and books, but every owl item sent served as a reminder that someone out there was thinking of and remembering our son. When words failed, an owl was more than enough. We tattooed owls on our bodies as if we needed a permanent reminder of the boy we would never forget. We became, as my father is known to call us, the Family of the Owl, connected by our love and longing for Oliver.

I spent that year being as selfish as I could. I made it a priority to feel my feelings as they came and made all choices based on the goal of simply getting through that first year as a relatively whole person. I wrote a lot. I did so in part to honour and remember Oliver, but also to honour and remember who I was after losing him. When I wasn't feeling and writing, I gave equal time to allowing myself to be distracted with trips, friends, work and sitting on the couch with my husband bingeing on nonsensical but necessary television.

> "Getting over it" is a misguided but hopefully well-intentioned notion forced upon the grieving by the unaffected world.

I did some silly out-of-character things that year, too, like a juice cleanse and zip-lining and maybe got too inebriated at a wedding when I saw a little baby boy. But I felt I'd earned a couple of stumbles on the path to healing. I was certain I was nailing this grief thing. I checked everything off the list I'd made in my head so that there was no way I'd find myself years down the line knocked out by some surprising issue that I had neglected. As I navigated that first year, I realised a simple fact: there would be nothing worse than getting over it. Surviving Oliver's death and pretending it was something I never had to think of or deal with again was an impossible conclusion. "Getting over it" is a misguided but hopefully well-intentioned notion forced upon the grieving by the unaffected world.

That's not reality. You don't get to create and carry a child for forty weeks and then just forget about him.

You will never be done dealing with that.

That is not how the world works. And that is definitely not how grief works. Grief is not linear. It's not a to-do list you can check off and pat yourself on the back for a job well done. Believe me; I tried. Grief is a circle, or a wild roller coaster ride or a heavy stone you learn to carry. Quite possibly, it is a beautiful mess that no single metaphor can encompass. For me, the remarkable thing about grief (if there can be anything remarkable about something so terrible and awful) is that it is never over. You are never done with it; grief comes with you wherever you go.

And so it should.

All those things I did that first year did not fix my grief. They could not solve my problem, because my problem is unsolvable. Yet, those steps were integral in getting me to where I am today.

Grief continues to pop up months, even years after loss. Sometimes I see it coming as an anniversary or holiday approaches, and other times it's entirely unexpected. A song will play on the radio, or I come across a picture of me pregnant and oblivious, and suddenly I am transported back to a time when Oliver was growing inside me. Just as instantly, I feel as if I have lost him all over again. The pain can be just as sharp as the moment the doctor told me that Oliver's heart had stopped beating inside me. When these moments arise and these feelings return, I allow myself to be momentarily swallowed up in sorrow.

> Grief is not linear; it's not a to-do list you can check off.

Instead of feeling the failure I thought I would, I feel gratitude. I'm so grateful grief comes with me because the loss of Oliver informs every decision I make, making my life better. Not better than it could have been with him, of course, but better perhaps than if I succumbed to the darker, less helpful facets of grief. One should never forget what it feels like to lose someone you love.

Just as I remember Oliver in my grief, I remember him as I surround myself with people I love. I choose to spend my time doing things that make me the happiest version of myself. Because of Oliver, I have a husband who I still think is cute and funny. Because of Oliver, I have three living children I would rather spend time with than anyone else (except for that cute husband). Because of Oliver, I recognise the good fortune I stumbled across in having family I would choose to be mine, even if we were not linked by genetics. Because of Oliver, I spend my days at the best job possible, with adults and children that are full of life and love and humour and honesty. Because of Oliver, I talk about my feelings and make sure to let the people I care about know exactly how much I love them.

Because of Oliver, because of grief, I have a great life. Oliver and the grief I choose to carry with me every day continue to remind me that we literally don't have time for anything less.

*Rachel Libby's first son Oliver was stillborn at forty weeks. In his honour, and in service to his brothers, she writes his story to ensure he stays present. When not writing, she spends her time teaching preschool. She lives in Sacramento, California, USA, with her husband and three children born after Oliver's death.*

# LIGHTING ANOTHER BIRTHDAY CANDLE

## ELIZABETH JONES

The year following the death of our son Benjamin was full of many firsts, not least his birthday. To think of experiencing that momentous date without him was unbelievably difficult. How could I approach that day with joy when it felt like a gigantic banner hung over my head reading, "HE IS NOT HERE!"? He is not here to celebrate this day. He is not here to jump out of bed in the morning full of joy and anticipation. He is not here to sit on our bed and eagerly open his presents. On Benjamin's four birthdays with us, we rejoiced that he had reached another milestone. Could we do that after his death? Could we continue to celebrate his birthday when he is not here?

Benjamin was born with hypoplastic left heart syndrome, a congenital heart defect. The left side of his heart never developed, so he was born with half a heart. Benjamin's prognosis was devastating. Without immediate surgical intervention, he would not survive. Living with that reality hovering in our minds, each day with him was a gift. In his four and a half short years of life, Benjamin endured seven open-heart surgeries and countless other procedures, all considered palliative surgeries. Despite the medical attention and his perseverance, Benjamin died.

His death has left an enormous hole in our family. We've been robbed of events when we can celebrate, such as Benjamin's achievements in school, sporting clubs, hobby clubs or any number of milestones children reach throughout their lifetime. This has made Benjamin's birthday even more meaningful. It's the one day that is just for Benjamin. Yet, we were at a loss as we approached Benjamin's fifth birthday, our first without him

**The lead-up to his birthday was worse than the day itself.**

here. The lead up to his birthday was worse than the day itself. Anxious thoughts crowded my mind. How would I feel? Would I want to be alone or with family? What would others say and do? Would they acknowledge Benjamin's birthday or quietly ignore the meaning behind the day? The weight of anticipation steadily grew as the day drew near, pressing down on me like a heavy burden with no way of finding relief. In the end, we, as a couple, made plans we thought would suit us, allowing ourselves complete flexibility to cancel those plans at any time.

The actual day was difficult, but also sadly beautiful. We visited the cemetery with my immediate family. We delivered gifts to Benjamin: blue (his favourite colour) garden toys, a windmill and a butterfly on a stake. We freshened up his gravesite and added beautiful blue flowers. Then we went out for breakfast at a local cafe. My husband, our younger son and I spent the afternoon at home by ourselves for some quiet time before my husband's immediate family came over for dinner. I had made a birthday cake shaped into a cricket bat, or as Benjamin would have said, "a bat and ball!" We sang happy birthday, and because his baby brother was too little, Benjamin's school-age cousins who were close to him happily blew out his candles. After cake, we sat together and told stories about Benjamin. We reflected on happy memories and shared those moments when he had brought each of us joy.

Benjamin was a little person who impacted not only us, as his parents, but our family and friends as well. A couple of family members, upon later reflection on that first birthday without Benjamin, confided how important they felt it was for our extended family to have the opportunity to get together to celebrate and remember Benjamin. They expressed how they appreciated the chance to sit together and share stories with a particular focus on allowing Benjamin's young cousins to be reminded of him. It was so meaningful for my husband and me to hear that our families understood the need to honour our precious child in this way. What may have been a simple statement to them made my heart swell with gratitude to know that they wanted to pass on their wonderful stories of Benjamin to their children. What a beautiful gift and how fitting for a birthday.

## We have learned to do whatever feels right.

As we grieve Benjamin, it continues to be important to my husband and me that our extended families set aside this one day, Benjamin's birthday, to commemorate his life. It's a challenging time of year for everyone to make time, as it is close to Christmas, and with family members living several hours away we know it requires effort on their part. For me, their love for Benjamin shines through more than anything else they can give or do for us when they prioritise his birthday.

Even though he is no longer physically here, there are many things my husband and I can do to celebrate Benjamin's birthday. We can spend time with family and friends who know our journey and recognise how important this day is for us. We might visit Benjamin's burial site or the beach that was a familiar and special place to him. We can volunteer at an organisation that is meaningful for us. We have learned to do whatever feels right. On his fifth birthday, we chose to honour Benjamin by doing something special on his behalf. We invited friends and family to participate by donating the money they would have spent on Benjamin's present. Collectively, we purchased three bikes for a family with a child spending a lengthy time in the hospital, as Benjamin had, connected to an artificial Berlin Heart. We hoped to share Benjamin's joy with this family during the Christmas season.

> I have realised there is no right or wrong way to celebrate my son's birthday.

I have realised there is no right or wrong way to celebrate my son's birthday. It will always be a hard and painful day, but I can and do celebrate Benjamin. He was here, and he lived for four amazing years. On his birthday, more than any other day, my husband and I can share that, with our hearts bursting with pride and love.

Each year on December 11, we focus on his life – rather than his death – and shout to all who will listen, "Benjamin was here, and he was our son!" We share about him with others. We remember him and tell of our love for him. We honour him quietly or boldly, on our own or with lots of people surrounding us. It is important for us to take the time to honour him. He will always be ours, and we are forever his.

*Elizabeth Jones is a speech pathologist who works with children with special needs. She is also a wife and mother to three children, two on earth and one in heaven. She hopes that by sharing her experience of losing her four-year-old son Benjamin she may inspire other bereaved parents on the same journey.*

# GRATEFUL AND GRIEVING

## RYAN THOMPSON

Aveline Mae was born unexpectedly on July 8 at 6:01pm – sixteen weeks before her expected due date. She was just twelve inches long and weighed one pound, seven and a half ounces. She was absolutely perfect. She was pink, moving around and clearly feisty. I was told she cried just before she was intubated. I have tried very hard to remember that, but I can't. As Aveline was born and being taken care of, her mother, Leah, was unconscious on an operating table having just undergone an emergency caesarean section. How I wish she could have seen her first daughter, her first child, in those moments.

I had no idea Aveline (Ava) would come into my world this way. Until that fateful day in the doctor's office, there was no reason for me to worry. In fact, I had taken much for granted when it came to Leah's pregnancy with Ava. Both before and during the pregnancy, we simply weren't in a good place. Our marriage was struggling, and we were having a difficult time digging ourselves out from under the issues that piled on top of us. I assumed, albeit naively, that Ava would be the miracle that would fix our relationship problems. It is fair to say that in my thirty years of life, I have faced my share of adversity. Every life lesson learned and every ounce of pain I felt could not have prepared me for what was in store.

We walked into the obstetrics and gynaecology office on the afternoon of July 8 expecting a quick routine check, and then we would continue on our way to dinner and a movie. I am guessing by the time we were in an exam room, it was close to 5:00pm. By 5:30pm, we were being rushed to the hospital in an ambulance because the ultrasound technicians discovered Ava's heart rate was dangerously low – in the fifties. In just forty minutes' time, Ava was born.

It was discovered quickly after Ava's birth that she had a heart defect that was causing her abnormally low heart rate. Doctors expected she should have been in far worse shape with a heart rate that low. Contrary to that expectation, she was pink, she was moving, and looked like a "healthy" premature baby. In a few hours, we were told Ava had third-degree heart block, a condition that breaks the electrical pathways in the heart. Ava's ventricles were pumping at a steady fifty-ish beats per minute, (normal heart rate for a newborn would be 120 to 160 beats per minute) because her heart muscles were doing so naturally. There was no electrical activity triggering her ventricles to beat at the rate her atria (the two upper cavities of the heart) were beating, which was much, much higher.

> Every life lesson learned and every ounce of pain I felt could not have prepared me for what was in store.

Her prematurity and her heart condition put Ava in a very grave situation. After her birth, I had thirty-five hours with my precious daughter before she died. She held my finger for a little while which made me so proud. Thankfully, we were able to be there when she died. At 4:42am on July 10, Aveline Mae passed away in her mother's arms.

It is my theory that men are often the silent types who don't talk much about things that bring them emotional pain. I was no different. I am not one to wear my heart on my sleeve or express my emotions freely when I am moved by anything: good or bad. Ava changed that completely. She changed a few things. Nothing has impacted me more than my Ava. Out of every person I have known in my life, I knew her the least amount of time. There isn't anyone who has altered my outlook on life as she did. Surprisingly, she has helped me work towards being a better man, a better husband and a better human being.

For what remains of this short essay, I will explain how my beautiful, perfect, amazing daughter changed my life for the better in just less than five months, from a man's perspective.

*Love.* I fell in love with Ava's mother, Leah. Our love has been tested in many ways, and in one aspect love was something I developed over time with her. With Ava, my love for her was instantaneous. As soon as I saw her, I was hooked. To know that someone lives because you helped create them is such a powerful feeling. I was drawn to her, afraid for her and absolutely desperate to save her. The love between a father and a daughter is an unbreakable link. Ava gave me that gift, even if I only experienced that link with her on this earth for such a short time. I will always know what that love feels like, and it is because of her. No matter how old I grow or where I am or what I do, I will always be a father who loves his daughter more than anything in the world. That brings me so much joy.

*Priorities.* Before Ava was born, my priorities were work, sorting through (but typically arguing about) the troubles in my marriage and staying sober. It isn't necessary to go into detail, but I am a recovering alcoholic and addict. This has played a role in the troubles in our marriage and played a much larger role in my struggles in life. I wasn't really a family man. I made money, but I didn't do well taking care of Leah the way a husband should. As I said before, I took for granted that Ava would be in my life forever and would solve all my problems. I had no idea she would help me in the way she did. I would give anything, and I mean absolutely anything, to receive these gifts without losing her. I ache that I learned these things because of her coming and going so quickly.

Although I was dealing with my own grief after Ava passed, I was programmed to take care of Leah and keep us afloat financially while focusing on what mattered. While I am not perfect, I am proud of the family of three we are. I need only Ava, Leah and me for all to be well in the world, and I will do all that is possible to protect that. Ava is such a prominent part of my life, and I try to act in her best interest and what I know (or hope) would make her proud. Because of that mindset, so many things that used to matter before just don't anymore.

> **Nothing has impacted me more than my Ava. I will never be the man I was before, nor should I be.**

*Fatherhood.* It's hard to know what to say, especially at first, about being a parent to an only child whom you also lost. I felt like I was given an amazing gift, but then it was just as swiftly taken away. It took time for me to accept that I would only be a father with Ava gone. I had no other options. Although I had a great deal of pride for who she was and the time we shared, there was no way for me to channel that because she was gone. Early on, I talked a lot about what I felt. I talked with Leah every day about how I was feeling, and I cried a lot. More than I ever thought was possible. By working through those feelings, I could reach a point where I understood that even though Ava was gone, she was still my daughter, and I was still her father; and I could always carry an immeasurable amount of pride in that. I am a father today. I can and will live my life as a proud father, even if I never have another child. Ava *is* my daughter, not *was* my daughter.

> I am a proud father, even if I never have another child. Ava is my daughter, not was my daughter.

*Compassion.* I don't mean to say that this is typical of every man. The majority of the time, I was previously emotionally affected by nothing and didn't really care about much either. If there was pain and suffering in the world or if another person in my life was going through something difficult, I would understand their situation, but I would not be affected by it. It's quite possible I wouldn't say anything either, most likely because I wouldn't know what to say. I can't tell you how much compassion I now have for others because of this journey. I never would have understood it today if it wasn't for Ava, but there is a great deal of honour in taking time to talk about difficult things with other people and take part in their pain. You never know how you can help them.

Very recently, a co-worker was diagnosed with cancer. She is a kind, thoughtful woman who was one of the first persons to talk to me and acknowledge my loss after I returned to work. Out of anyone, she knew me the least. I know without hesitation, if it wasn't for Ava and my journey so far, I never would have gone out of my way to be one of the few people to talk with her and do what I could to support her. The day she announced her diagnosis, I spoke with her. I did that, because I knew what it was like to be in such a lonely place and how helpful it can be to have someone talk with you and just be there as someone who genuinely cares. I was so full of joy that day. I pictured what Ava would have thought of me when she saw me do that.

*Hope.* To bring this to a close, I can't begin to express how many times I have felt completely worthless after losing Ava. I felt like there was nothing I had a purpose for in the world once I lost her. The truth is, those days will continually come and go, as I suspect will be the case long after I write this. I don't lose hope because I know that one bad day doesn't mean the remainder of my life will be awful. This journey and this pain will do nothing but make me a stronger, better person.

Without question, Aveline Mae changed my life for the better. I lost someone amazing who taught me so much, in so little time. I will never be the man I was before, nor should I be.

*Ryan Thompson is a financial analyst in southwestern Michigan. When he's not working, he enjoys making people laugh and spending time with his wife, Leah, and their dog, Zoey. He's passionate about fatherhood and bringing honour to his first-born daughter, Aveline.*

# SECTION TEN

# RESOURCES

## WHERE TO GO FROM HERE

# WE ARE HERE FOR YOU
## SUGGESTIONS FROM BEREAVED PARENTS

The following section in its original form was published in the book *Grieving Parents* by Nathalie Himmelrich. We include it here again as a resource.

> *If people are not willing to share their hearts, there is (this) isolation. Sharing will open up an environment where more people feel safe doing it and it won't be as hard to grieve organically. – Lori Ennis*

One statement that I heard over and over from my interviewees in response to what they would want other bereaved parents to remember was: *"You are not alone"*. The death of a child often feels devastating and isolating. Dealing with people's lack of understanding, well-meant suggestions and cliché statements will be additional challenges you must deal with. We offer you these gems of wisdom bereaved parents who have walked the path you're walking now would want to gift you. Take what fits for you.

**WE ENCOURAGE YOU TO...**
- Seek help earlier
- Make your own decisions
- Take more time, take more photos of your baby
- Seek support when wanting to get pregnant again
- Face fears sooner rather than later
- Hold a ceremony to celebrate your child
- Worry less about what others think

## GEMS OF WISDOM

*We are here for three reasons: to give and receive love, to learn compassion and to learn forgiveness. – Tamara Gabriel*

**Self-Care.** Listen to your own needs, grieve, share, read books, accept what is, ponder your spiritual and religious beliefs, remember you will never be the same person.

**Relationships.** Give each other time, accept how your partner is grieving, accept how he/she is, spend time as a couple, stick together and don't give up, practice tolerance and honesty, be patient, show emotions openly, accept and allow your partner's feelings.

*The paradox of allowing and seeing your partner's feelings needs to happen at the same time as wanting to bang his chest and scream and wanting him to be what you want him to be. – Martina Sandles*

**Be understanding and accepting...**

*I will never understand how he is feeling; I will never understand it from his perspective. I'm just not him. He will never understand a miscarriage, because he just is not me. There is nothing that can change that. – Lori Ennis*

**Therapy.** Go to therapy earlier, try another therapist if one isn't working, take time grieving, talk about the child/baby, show emotions openly, accept feelings and allow them.

**Your environment.** Befriend someone who has gone through this experience (another grieving parent), find supportive people, do not listen to what others are saying or suggesting if their comments are less than helpful, prepare for uneasiness of society.

**Selecting an entrusted audience.**

*We choose who we want to be open with. There are just people who don't rate being open to. – John Ennis*

**Your baby/child.** Hold the baby, take photos, make memories, listen to your own needs, do what it is you need, talk about the baby or child.

*The experience with Hannah has opened me to love in a way that I never thought I was able to conceive or open to. This stays with me to this day. – Martina Sandles*

healing is
a reflection
of self-love

# HEALING TOGETHER
## GRIEVING PARENTS SUPPORT NETWORK

**The Grieving Parents Support Network (GPSN)** is a community for bereaved parents and family members who have lost a child. The intent is to support and uplift. It is a safe space where bereaved parents can come, read, feel understood, rest, share, find information and resources, learn, process grief and connect with other bereaved parents. The GPSN is also a place for friends and family wanting to support bereaved parents in their journey of grief and child loss. We invite all who want to come to sit, hold space for them and find out how to tend to the grieving heart. *Visit www.grievingparents.net for guidance on…*

### Supporting Yourself

From music to movies and books, articles and online groups – we list many resources that have helped other bereaved parents under Resources.

### Supporting Others

Supporters help parents survive this most horrendous time in their lives, if they really know how to be supportive. If you want to help anyone, then you must be able to deal with parental bereavement in a better way. We invite you to begin to explore how under Start Here.

### Online Support

We provide a list of resources that includes various support organizations. Find the one that is right for your individual needs under Resources.

## Community Support

The GPSN also offers community-led projects to support your journey from healthy grieving to healthy healing. Find those listed under Projects.

## Peer Support

We invite you to join our private May We All Heal peer support group on Facebook, a community of bereaved parents and family members who have lost a child. Here we support one another through activities and conversations about various topics, join at www.facebook.com/groups/MayWeAllHeal.

## Professional Support

Nathalie Himmelrich offers personal one-on-one support for grieving parents, individually or as a couple, and other family members. She also facilitates group seminars and workshops. For professional counselling and coaching, visit www.nathaliehimmelrich.com.

**www.grievingparents.net**
**www.facebook.com/GrievingParents.net**

# DONATE
## SUPPORT OUR MISSION

Our mission is to normalise grief and validate grieving parents' emotions. We strive to support bereaved parents, assure them that they and their feelings are "normal" and allow them to feel understood. More than anything, we want to let them know they are not alone.

The Grieving Parents Support Network (GPSN) aims to come alongside bereaved parents with our written work, online resources and peer support groups to gently carry them forward in this life-long journey of loss. To this end, we share our own stories of loss and hope with parents grieving the loss of a child of any age.

As a not-for-profit, all GPSN contributors and moderators generously volunteer their time and talent as labours of love. Nonetheless, we carry the moderate costs of an online presence and costs related to design, production and shipping for each book.

Your donations help the charity arm of GPSN provide sponsored copies of our resource books to hospitals, bereavement centres, grief retreats and other not-for-profit organisations.

Each book purchase, sponsored copy and direct donation helps us gift books to the individuals who most need it – bereaved parents in the earliest stages of their grief. We thank you for partnering with us to make this mission possible.

**www.grievingparents.net/donate**

healing
doesn't mean
denying
or forgetting
the past

# RESOURCE BOOKS FOR GRIEVING PARENTS

We invite you to explore each of our books below. We offer these as resources for grieving parents and their family and friends offering support. Purchase a copy to assist you in your own grief journey or to support a bereaved loved one or friend experiencing grief.

### Das erste Jahr nach dem Verlust meines Kindes überleben: Persönliche Geschichten von trauernden Eltern

Essays von 26 Eltern, die über die Art und Weise berichten, wie sie persönliche Herausforderungen nach dem Tod ihres Kindes gemeistert haben.

Erhältlich als Taschenbuch und E-Book.

### Grieving Parents: Surviving Loss as a Couple

The book focuses on the effect of parental bereavement and describes five steps to survive grieving as a couple.

Available as softcover and ebook.

## Trauernde Eltern: Wie ein Paar den Verlust eines Kindes überlebt

Das Buch konzentriert sich auf die Wirkung der elterlichen Trauer und beschreibt fünf Schritte, um Trauer als Paar zu überleben.

Erhältlich als Taschenbuch und E-Book.

## May We All Heal Playbook: For Creative Healing After Loss

Use your creativity to channel grief into healing with this artfully designed playbook that combines the benefits of creative expression with journaling.

Available as softcover, hardcover and ebook.

**To donate books** to your local hospital, bereavement centre, support group or other organisation to honour the memory of your child, we invite you to review our Memory Packages.

Personalised dedication stickers include your baby or child's name hand-lettered by the author.

www.grievingparents.net/memory-packages

## We provide special bulk discounts

when you order five or more copies for bereavement organisations, support groups, hospitals, grief retreats or other similar not-for-profit purposes.

www.grievingparents.net/donate-books

*For additional details or special requests, please send an email to info@grievingparents.net*

# AFTERWORD
## AN INVITATION

It doesn't interest me to know
what you do for a living.
I want to know
who your heart
had to say goodbye to
way too soon
and if you dare to tell me
his or her name.

It doesn't interest me to know
how old you are.
I want to know
if you risk being told
"isn't it time to move on"
by remaining authentic
in your expression
of the longing for your child.

It doesn't interest me to know
where you live.
I want to know
if you have touched
the centre of your grief
if your heart has been opened by loss
I want to know if you are prepared
to go there as I sit here
with you, holding your hand.

It doesn't interest me to know
what awards you've achieved.
I want to know
if you are brave enough
to meet your own vulnerability.
I want to know
if you can sit with the pain
mine or you own
without moving to hide it
or fade it
or fix it.

It doesn't interest me to know
what or where you have studied.
I want to know
if you do all you can
to feel joy again
and not feel guilty.

It doesn't interest me to know
whether the story you're telling
is true.
I want to know
if you can disappoint another
to remain true
to yourself;
if you can bear the accusation
of "being stuck in grief"
and not betray your desire
to keep the memory
of your child alive.

It doesn't interest me to know
how much money you have.
I want to know
if you can get up
after a night of despair
and grief

and do what needs to be done
to look after yourself.
Even if that is
going back to bed.

It doesn't interest me
who you know
or how you came here to be.
I want to know
if you can stand
at the centre of longing
and sadness
with me
and not shrink back.

To know the company of others
who've experienced what you've experienced
is what can sustain you in your empty moments.

I want you to know you are not alone.
I want to know you.

*Inspired by The Invitation by Oriah Mountain Dreamer*

# GLOSSARY OF TERMS

**Berlin Heart** – An implantable device that takes over the work of one or both sides of a child's heart.

**Born still** – See stillbirth.

**Cannula** – A thin tube inserted into a vein or body cavity to administer medicine, drain off fluid or insert a surgical instrument.

**Cold cot** – See CuddleCot™.

**Congenital heart defect or disease** – A problem in the structure of the heart that is present at birth.

**CuddleCot™ (cold cot)** – A cooling pad that is put in a cot and keeps the baby's body temperature down, removing the need to take the baby to the mortuary, meaning the baby can stay with the family longer.

**Dilation and Curettage (D&C)** – A procedure sometimes performed after a miscarriage in order to remove tissue from the uterus.

**Doppler** – Device used to listen to a baby's heartbeat while in utero.

**Empty Cradle** – See Leere Wiege.

**Exchange transfusion** – This procedure involves slowly removing the person's blood and replacing it with fresh donor blood or plasma.

**Fob** – See key fob.

**HELLP syndrome** – HELLP (Haemolysis, Elevated Liver enzymes, Low Platelet count) syndrome is often considered a variant or complication of preeclampsia. Treatment usually requires delivery of the baby, even if the baby is premature.

**IV** – Intravenous. A device used to allow a fluid such as blood or a liquid medication to flow directly into a patient's veins.

**IVF** – In Vitro Fertilization. An assisted reproductive technology where eggs are extracted and then fertilised by sperm in a laboratory dish before being implanted in the uterus.

**Hypoplastic left heart syndrome** – Complex and rare congenital heart defect present at birth in which the left side of the heart is severely underdeveloped and can't effectively pump blood to the body.

**Key fob** – A piece of material or other ornament to which a group of keys is fastened.

**Kindness Project** – A way for families to honour loved ones who have died by performing random, and usually anonymous, acts of kindness in their communities.

**Leere Wiege (Empty Cradle)** – This course, offered in Germany and Austria, provides postpartum exercise combined with grief support for mothers whose child died prior to, during or shortly after birth.

**Mandala** – A circular figure representing the universe in Hindu and Buddhist symbolism.

**Miscarriage** – Death of a baby in the womb, usually before 20 weeks' gestation. See also silent miscarriage.

**Missed abortion** – See silent miscarriage.

**Missed miscarriage** – See silent miscarriage.

**MISShare** – A parent-led network that provides resources and support to parents after the death of their baby.

**Montessori** – Method of education based on self-directed activity, hands-on learning and collaborative play.

**Neonatologist** – Doctor specialised in the medical care of newborn infants.

**NICU** – Neonatal Intensive Care Unit. Intensive care unit specialising in care of ill or premature newborn infants.

**Obstetrician-Gynaecologist** – Doctor specialised in women's health.

**Perforated bowel** – Hole all the way through the wall of the large intestine.

**Potters syndrome** – A serious and often fatal condition where a baby's kidneys do not properly develop in utero. As a result, there is a lack of amniotic fluid. The lack of amniotic fluid causes the baby to be compressed by the uterine walls and also inhibits lung development.

**Premature** – Birth of a baby prior to 37 weeks' gestation.

**PTSD** – Post-Traumatic Stress Disorder. A condition of persistent mental and emotional stress occurring as a result of injury or severe psychological shock, typically involving disturbance of sleep and constant vivid recall of the experience, with dulled responses to others and to the outside world.

**Rainbow baby** – A baby born after the death of a previous baby because of miscarriage, stillbirth or infant death. The term comes from the idea that after a storm, a rainbow appears.

**Rh Disease (Isoimmunisation)** – A serious condition caused by an incompatibility between the blood of a mother and that of her baby. It can occur when the mother is Rh-negative and her baby is Rh-positive.

**Sabbatical** – A period of paid leave from work, typically for focused study or travel.

**Silent miscarriage** – When the baby has died or failed to develop but the mother's body has not actually miscarried the foetus (also called delayed miscarriage or delayed/missed abortion).

**Spotify** – A digital music service that provides access to music, including ready-made playlists and newly released albums.

**Still mother (still parent)** – Term used in the child and baby loss community to describe a mother or parent with no living children.

**Still Standing Magazine** – An online magazine with articles by bereaved parents about surviving loss and infertility.

**Stillbirth (stillborn baby)** – Birth of a baby that has died in the womb, usually after 20 weeks' gestation.

**Swaddling blanket** – Cloth or blanket used to wrap a newborn to soothe and quieten the baby for sleep.

**TED Talks** – TED talks initially began as a conference on Technology, Entertainment and Design. Now, TED talks include short videos from expert speakers on nearly all topics ranging from science to global issues.

**Toxoplasmosis** – A parasitic disease resulting from infection by the common Toxoplasma gondii parasite. It can cause serious complications for infants born to infected mothers.

**Vasa Praevia** – A condition in which the baby's blood vessels run across the birth canal and risk rupturing, causing foetal haemorrhage.

**Wave of Light** – This is a remembrance project that takes place on October 15th of each year. At 7pm in their time zone, people around the world light a candle in remembrance of the babies they've lost, creating a continual wave of light around the world.

# FROM THE AUTHOR'S DESK

## NATHALIE HIMMELRICH

As an author, I process my experiences through writing. I have written a number of resources, including articles and books, to support the grief experiences of parents after child loss. I also facilitate workshops, speak at retreats and provide keynote presentations for grief conferences for English and German speaking audiences.

My professional background is as a relationship coach and grief recovery expert. I love to help people find inspiration for healthy grieving and healing through my role as a Transformational Coach and Counsellor. My passion is to write and rethink human behaviour and emotion.

As a bereaved mother myself, I believe supportive relationships – intimate and with other support people – are the foundation for a healthy grieving experience. As part of the vision for support and better understanding of the grieving process – especially for bereaved parents – I've created the Grieving Parents Support Network. I hope bereaved parents will find the community and support they need through that network. Our regular not-for-profit projects encourage healthy grieving and healing.

For inquiries regarding interviews, seminars, workshops or mourning accompaniment, or for corrections in this book, please write to info@grievingparents.net.

Author: www.nathaliehimmelrich.com
www.facebook.com/NathalieHimmelrich
www.instagram.com/mymissbliss
www. twitter.com/nhimmelrich

# your loss is unique
# Your grief too

We hope this book speaks to your experience
and is helpful to you as you journey through
the grief of child loss.

We would be very grateful if you would
share a review so other grieving parents
can learn about this book.

www.grievingparents.net/reviews

CPSIA information can be obtained
at www.ICGtesting.com
Printed in the USA
FSOW03n1920181017
40076FS